The European Qurʾān

The European Qurʾān

Encounters with the Holy Text of Islam from the Ninth to the Twentieth Century

Edited by Jan Loop and Naima Afif

welt museum wien

DE GRUYTER

Contents

Preface

Jonathan Fine, Director Weltmuseum Wien

The Qur'ān is the Holy Book of Islam, which God revealed to the Prophet Muhammad in the seventh century CE. For Muslims it is much more than a book – it is a total work of art: recitation, architecture, poetry, calligraphy, and mysticism. Many Muslims believe that its sacred words cannot be translated. Quotes from the Qur'ān are emblazoned on countless buildings and beautifully crafted artefacts, many of which found their way to the West. In the Middle Ages and the Renaissance, precious Qur'ān manuscripts were brought to Europe for many different reasons. Here, they were studied by scholars and collected by art-loving rulers.

The Qur'ān's role and importance, however, changed over the centuries. The Enlightenment, for instance, read it as a celebration of reason and natural religion, while the Romantics praised it as a literary masterpiece. In the nineteenth century, European countries conquered many mainly Muslim lands in India, Southeast Asia, and Africa, giving rise to new prejudices against Islam and the Qur'ān. Unlike many European colonial powers that repressed Muslims in the territories they ruled, the Austro-Hungarian Empire adopted the *Islamgesetz* ('Islam Act') in 1912. The law recognized Islam as an official religion of the Empire and granted Muslims the same rights as adherents of the other recognized faiths.

This publication is conceived in tandem with an exhibition at the Weltmuseum Wien and explores the role of the Qur'ān in European culture and identity since the early Middle Ages. Both are the result of a fruitful and profound collaboration with the Synergy Grant Project 'The European Qurʾān. Islamic Scripture in European Religion and Culture 1150–1850 (EuQu)'. EuQu examines the role of the Qurʾān in the intellectual, religious, and cultural life of Europe in the Middle Ages and the early modern period; it is funded by the European Research Council (ERC) in the framework of 'Horizon 2020: EU Programme for Research and Innovation' (grant agreement no. 810141). The leading institutions in this research consortium are the Spanish National Research Council (CSIC), the University of Naples L'Orientale (UNO), the University of Copenhagen, and the University of Nantes (UN).

I would like to thank everyone who contributed to the exhibition and this publication, especially the authors of the essays assembled here, the artists, Ruh al-Alam and Marwan Shahin, and Madinah Javed, Qurʾān reciter, as well as the institutions supporting the exhibition with loans and digital material. I am also most grateful to Jan Loop and his colleagues of the EuQu project, as well as to Tobias Mörike, our 'interface' to the research project, who, together with Naima Afif, a post-doctoral researcher at EuQu, curated the exhibition.

Gerhard Veigel was responsible for the elegant exhibition design, Marianne Stålhös was our graphic designer, Susanne Mendez oversaw the conservation of museum objects, Daniel Stevens was our English editor, Haggag Ali, Mustafa Al-Slaiman, and Uli Nickel produced the Arabic and German translations, Hanin Hannouch performed editing of the Arabic text. Neslihan Yakut and Hind Hafuda organised the educational programs and tours of the exhibition, and Elisabeth Kainberger of our exhibition management department ensured the smooth installation.

We are most thankful to the Weltmuseum Wien Friends, who generously supported this publication. I sincerely hope it will inspire readers to reflect on the Qurʾān, its ideas, and the integral part it has long played in Europe's intellectual, religious, and cultural life.

The Qur'ān in European History and Culture: an Introduction

Jan Loop, University of Copenhagen and New York University Abu Dhabi
Naima Afif, University of Copenhagen

The Qur'ān and Islam are traditionally seen as Europe's 'other', an antithesis to its self-narrative of cultural achievements: the Enlightenment, secularisation, and religious tolerance. Some claim that Islam in general and the Qur'ān in particular are alien to Europe's culture and political institutions. Developed as part of a large European-funded research project, this exhibition endeavours to counter this popular belief and to tell a different story by documenting the role the Qur'ān has played in the formation of culture, religion, scholarship, and politics in Europe. Our aim is to create a stimulating and thought-provoking exhibition, discussing the role of the Qur'ān in European history and the various transformations of Islam's sacred text when it was copied, translated, interpreted, and transmitted both within and across boundaries of language and belief.

Acquiring the Qur'ān – stealing, copying, buying, gifting

The acquisition of manuscripts posed a major difficulty to Christians interested in the Qur'ān. In many cases, Europeans acquired manuscripts peacefully through networks of trade, diplomacy, and scholarship. However, religious prohibition and suspicions about their intentions made it difficult for Christians to buy Qur'ān manuscripts. 'Looting' or 'stealing' were often the only possibilities for European scholars, collectors, and libraries to come into possession of Qur'āns and other Islamic manuscripts in the early modern period.

Since the Middle Ages and throughout the early modern period, large collections of Arabic, Turkish, and Persian manuscripts were looted by Christians, often during and after military confrontations with Islamic rulers and empires.

Sultan Moulay Zaydan (1603–27), for example, possessed a large private collection of manuscripts. In 1612, while facing the progress of one of his political opponents, Moulay Zaydan requested the services of a French merchant and consul to ship his belongings, including his entire library, from Safi to Agadir. The merchant, however, tried to escape with the cargo and the stolen ship was captured by the Spanish fleet. The sultan's collection became the property of Philip III of Spain and was transferred to the Royal Library of El Escorial, one of the most important repositories of Arabic manuscripts in Europe.

This was not a singular event, though: when the Habsburg Emperor Charles V conquered Tunis in 1535, his soldiers brought back numerous manuscripts, among them large numbers of Qurʾāns. Many of them were used by sixteenth-century scholars and can still be found in libraries all over Europe. Moreover, manuscripts looted during the so-called 'Great Turkish War' (1683–99) form the base of some of the richest collections of Arabic and Ottoman-Turkish manuscripts in Italian (Bologna), German (Dresden, Leipzig), and Austrian (Vienna) libraries, which consist almost exclusively of *Türkenbeute* (literally, 'Turkish booty').

Other manuscripts were acquired by European Christians travelling in the Islamic world. The Dominican scholar and missionary Riccoldo da Montecroce (1243–1320), author of a widely read refutation of the Qurʾān, for example, purchased an Arabic Qurʾān copied in Syria and filled the margins with notes in Latin. Other pieces, like some very rare old manuscripts in Copenhagen, Paris, St. Petersburg, Gotha etc., had been taken from a depot of the ʿAmr mosque in al-Fustat, old Cairo. Such precious pieces often served as gifts among European dignitaries and scholars (**fig. 1**).

Another way to get into possession of Qurʾān manuscripts was to copy them by hand. In Europe, the Qurʾān and other Middle Eastern manuscripts were copied not only by Muslims, but also by Christians, Jews and converts, transcending identity boundaries and writing practices. In the Habsburg borderlands of Spain and other parts of Europe, Muslim slaves and captives often acted as scribes. Reflecting such a diversity, copies of the Qurʾān were written in various scripts, including Arabic calligraphy, Arabic in a European setting, and Hebrew (**fig. 2**).

In medieval Iberia, for example, several testimonies indicate that female slaves as well as upper-class women played a decisive role in the history of the Qurʾān in Europe, either by taking part in the production of Qurʾānic

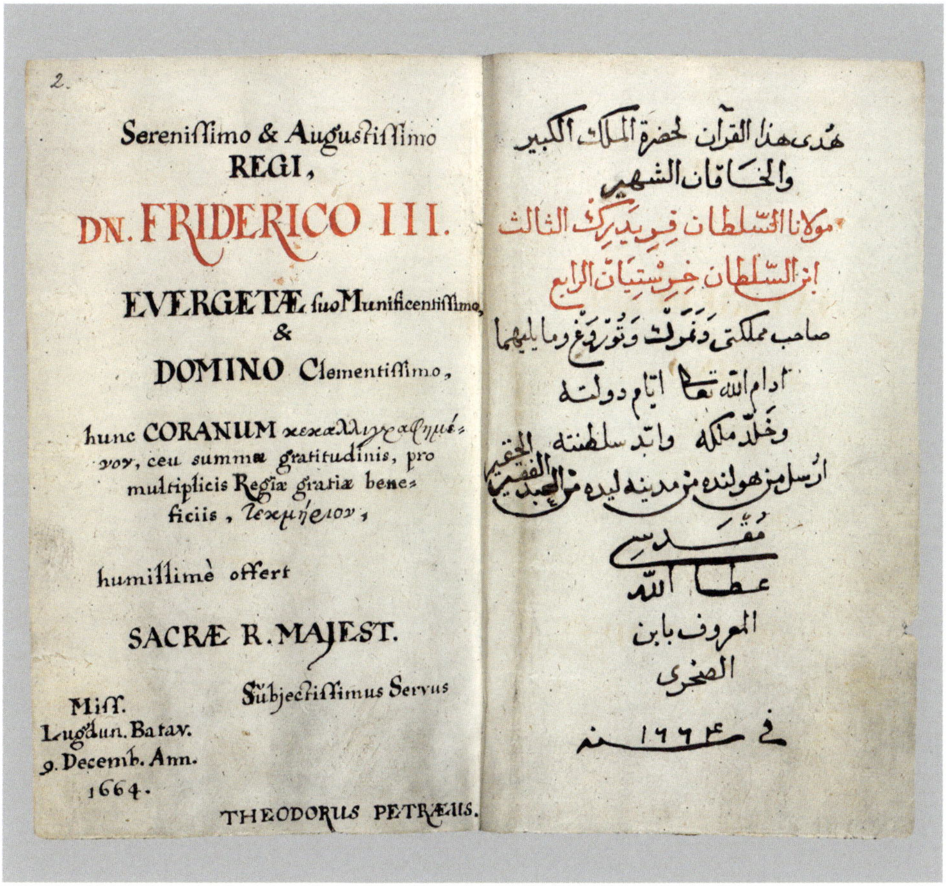

Fig. 1: Qurʾān manuscript gifted to Frederik III, King of Denmark, by Theodor Petræus (d.1672), Dano-German orientalist, with dedication in Latin and Arabic. Royal Library København, Cod. Arab. 19, title page with dedication

manuscripts or by engaging with Qurʾānic scholarship. According to the tenth-century historian Ibn al-Fayyād, there were one hundred women just in Cordoba copying Qurʾān manuscripts in Kufic script in his time. In the same period, Lubna of Cordoba, a female mathematician and poet, headed the library of Caliph Abd Ar-Rahman III, the largest library in the medieval Islamic world. The Andalusian Muslim, jurist and theologian ibn Ḥazm (tenth/eleventh century) attested that his father's slave women taught him about the Qurʾān, poetry, and calligraphy when he was a boy.

Informants, mediators, and knowledge brokers of Islam

Muslim minorities in Europe – mainly in Iberia and the former Ottoman territories in Central and Eastern Europe – but also prisoners of war, slaves, merchants, diplomats and Eastern Christians played a central role in the history of the Qurʾān in Europe. In many cases, Muslims or Arab Christians in Europe acted as translators or scribes, helping Christians to understand difficult Qurʾānic passages or to copy Islamic texts.

In the early sixteenth century, Rome became the epicentre for the study of various previously unknown languages in Europe. It was also a hub that connected the Western and Eastern Christian worlds. Ethiopic, Syriac, and Arabic-speaking Christians would gather in Rome and bring with them linguistic and cultural expertise as well as numerous manuscripts. Nevertheless, Rome hosted not only Eastern Christians as linguistic and cultural mediators. Collaborations between Christians, Muslims, and converts are well-documented. A translation of the Qurʾān, commissioned by Egidio da Viterbo (1469–1532), was produced in a joint effort by Juan Gabriel (dates unknown), a learned convert from Teruel in Aragon, and the Moroccan diplomat and captive al-Hassan ibn Muhammad al-Wazzan (1494–c.1554), known as Leo Africanus. A Muslim judge from Segovia, Içe de Gebir (or: Isa de Gebir), prepared a preliminary Castilian translation of the Qurʾān, which John of Segovia (d. 1458) used as the basis of his Latin translation of the Qurʾān between 1455 and 1458.

In a number of cases, captured and enslaved Muslims were forced into these collaborations. The Catalan theologian and missionary Ramon Llull (1232–1315) received instructions in Arabic from a Muslim slave for many years and they also read the Qurʾān together. The unnamed slave later committed suicide after a violent encounter with Llull, allegedly over the divinity of the Qurʾān and the prophethood of Jesus Christ. The learned Ottoman captive Ibrahim Dervīş assisted the Viennese orientalist Sebastian Tengnagel (d. 1636) for years as a scribe and informant, all the while living as a prisoner under precarious conditions.

In Iberia, for example, *Moriscos* – Muslims forcefully converted to Christianity – were in need of their own translations and interpretations of the Qurʾānic text. They collected, circulated, and copied Arabic texts, annotated them, and produced Qurʾān translations in *aljamia*, Spanish written in Arabic. Moriscos and Tatar Muslims translated the Qurʾān into their spoken languages, writing their texts in Spanish or Polish yet in Arabic script. The *Tefsir of the Tatars*, the earliest translation of the entire Qurʾān into Polish in 1723 in the Grand Duchy of Lithuania, is a wonderful example of this process. In the manuscript, the Qurʾān

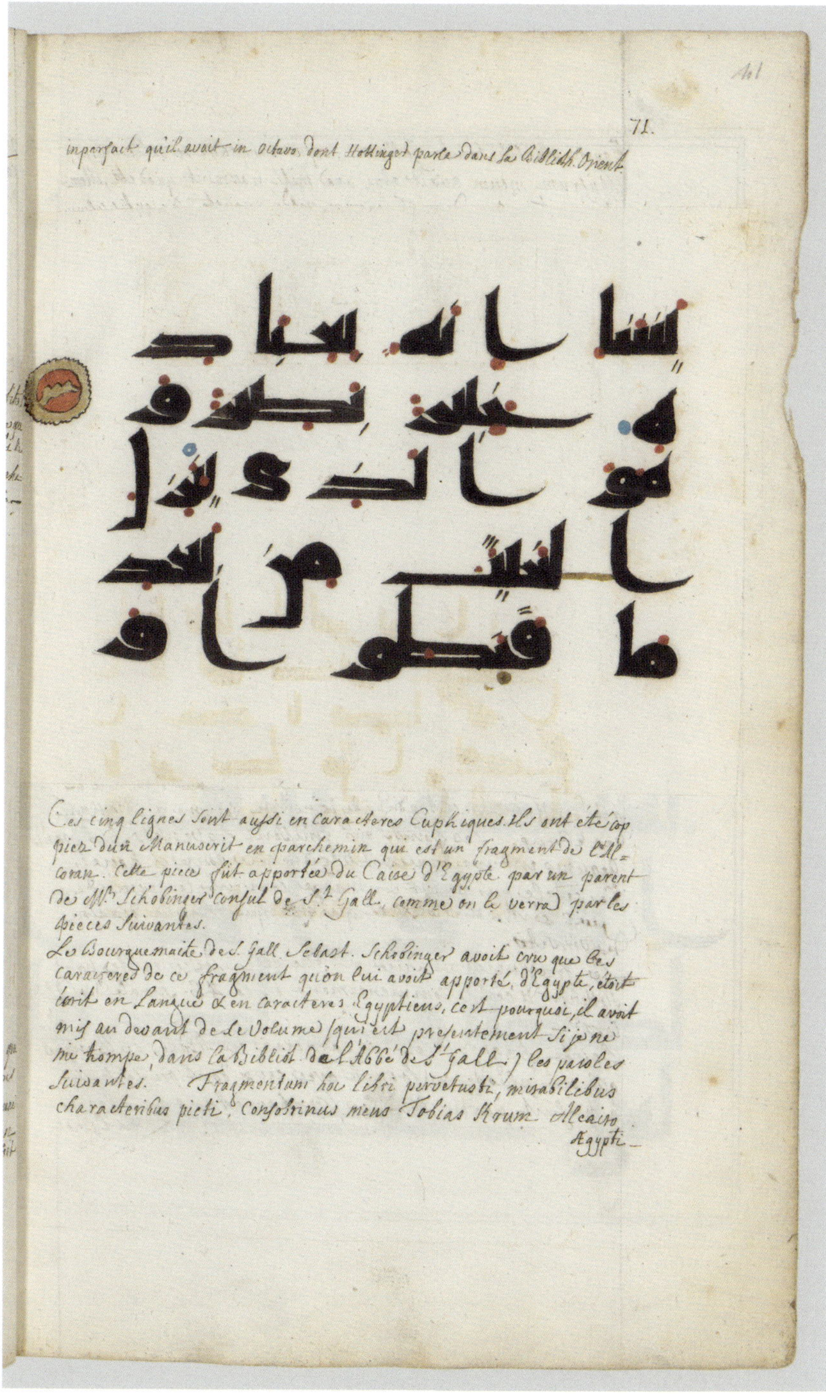

Fig. 2: Louis Bourguet's facsimile copy of a Kufic Qurʾān fragment. Bibliothèque nationale de France, Nouvelles acquisitions françaises, Ms 891, fol.41r

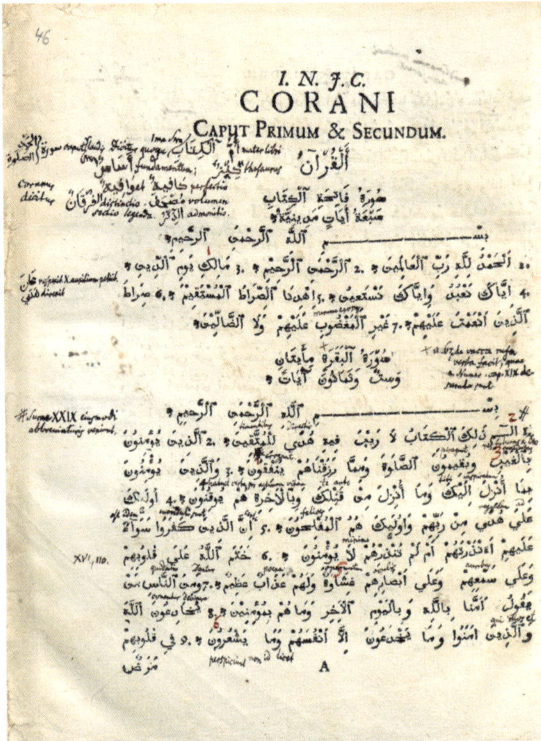

Fig. 3: Edition of the Qurʾān in Arabic by Abraham Hinckelmann with annotations by different students and teachers of Arabic (Hamburg, 1694). University Library Rostock, Ms orient. 101, fols. 45v–46r

in Arabic is written horizontally and the Polish translation in Arabic script runs diagonally between the lines.

However, we can find such linguistic and cultural brokers not only in southern and eastern Europe: in the early eighteenth century, two Arabic-speaking Christians from Syria offered their scholarly services to students of the Collegium Orientale Theologicum, an educational institution for future missionaries in Halle, Germany. Their Latinised names were Salomon Negri (Sulaymān b. Yaʿqūb al-Shāmī al-Ṣāliḥāni) (c.1665–1729) and Rali Carolus Dadichi (Shukrallāh al-Dādīkhī) (c.1694–1734). Their textbook for teaching was the Qurʾān (see **fig. 3**). The Rostock University Library holds a complete Latin translation of the Qurʾān in their name. Unfortunately, the details of this translation remain unclear.

The Qur'ān and European oriental scholarship

European scholars and writers used their knowledge of the Qur'ān and Islam in general for many different reasons. A constant concern was 'to know their enemy'. While traveling across Spain in 1142/3, Peter the Venerable, Abbot of Cluny (d.1156), commissioned an English translator of Arabic texts, Robert of Ketton (1110–c.60), with the translation of the Qur'ān into Latin in order to support the Christian struggle against Muslims. The resulting translation would remain the most widely read and used Qur'ān translation for the next 500 years. It was printed in Basel in 1543/50 and was further translated into Italian, German, Hebrew, and Dutch. The National Library of France holds one of the oldest handwritten copies of this translation. Like many translators after him, Ketton made use of Islamic commentary literature (*tafsīr*). His Latin translation was intended to convey both the meaning and elevated style of the Qur'ān.

In the following centuries, a great number of attempts were made to replace Ketton's version with a new, more literal translation. Many of these works – such as the translations by Içe de Gebir and John of Segovia (d.1485) mentioned above, or the one produced by Johann Zechendorff (1662) – were never printed. In 1647, André Du Ryer published the first direct translation from Arabic to French, and in 1698, Ludovico Marracci published his groundbreaking Latin translation in Padua. Even then, Marracci's main objective was to better understand Islam and the Qur'ān for missionary and polemical purposes.

Although European Jews certainly had some interest in the Qur'ān, there is no evidence that they produced any translation before the early modern period. In pre-modern times, however, Jews in Europe became more engaged with the Qur'ān and translated it into Hebrew and Spanish. Instead of the original Arabic, however, these Jewish translations were based on Christian translations and retranslations of the Qur'ān into vernacular languages.

Particularly since the Reformation, scholars had been consulting the Qur'ān for various other purposes, most importantly as a textbook to learn Arabic. Arabic was considered a close relative, indeed a dialect, of Hebrew, the original language of the Christian Old Testament. In the wake of the Reformation, Biblical scholars who wished to read the original Hebrew texts would often use Arabic in order to understand rare Hebrew words and phrases.

The Qur'ān was considered the norm and standard of Arabic, indeed a linguistic archive. Thomas Erpenius, the author of a groundbreaking Arabic grammar from 1613, is said to have read the Qur'ān four times, combing it each time for some new grammatical points. In schools, universities, and private settings,

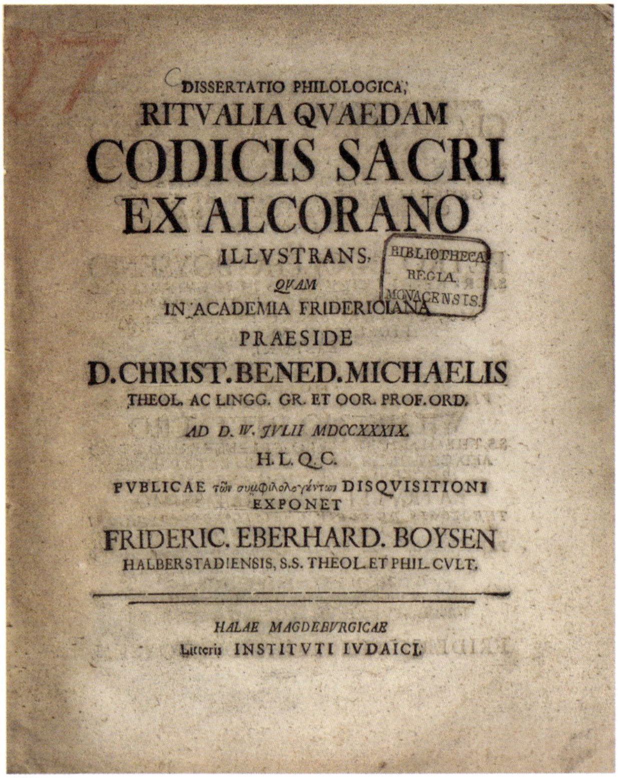

DISSERTATIO PHILOLOGICA,
RITVALIA QVAEDAM
CODICIS SACRI
EX ALCORANO
ILLVSTRANS,
QVAM
IN ACADEMIA FRIDERICIANA
PRAESIDE
D. CHRIST. BENED. MICHAELIS
THEOL. AC LINGG. GR. ET OOR. PROF. ORD.
AD D. IV. IVLII MDCCXXXIX.
H. L. Q. C.
PVBLICAE τῶν συμφιλολογούντων DISQVISITIONI
EXPONET
FRIDERIC. EBERHARD. BOYSEN
HALBERSTADIENSIS, S.S. THEOL. ET PHIL. CVLT.

HALAE MAGDEBVRGICAE
Litteris INSTITVTI IVDAICI.

Fig. 4: Christian Benedict Michaelis, *Dissertatio philologica ritualia quaedam codicis sacri ex alcorano illustrans* (Halle, 1739), title page

scholars used Qurʾāns and individual suras to learn and teach Arabic. In the seventeenth century, Protestant scholars published numerous Qurʾān excerpts for teaching purposes, so-called *Specimens* that contained editions of one or two suras in Arabic and Latin.

Nevertheless, the Qurʾān was not only used as an archive of the Arabic language to better understand the Hebrew language of the Old Testament. In the late seventeenth and early eighteenth century, the Qurʾān was also read to gather information about certain rituals, customs, and practices mentioned in the Bible, as well as about animals and plants, or even to understand the style of certain books, such as the Song of Solomon (**fig. 4**). Among scholars, Qurʾān manuscripts, particularly old ones in Kufic or Hijazi script, were also used to document the development of Semitic scripts and alphabets. The Qur'ān was, in other words, used as a cultural, religious, literary, and linguistic archive of the Biblical world.

The Qur'ān in European religion and politics

Chained to the stake on a pyre of his own books, the Spanish physician and polymath Miguel Servet was burnt in Geneva on 27 October 1553. Servet had provoked the ire of Jean Calvin and the Genevan authorities with a couple of publications. He argued that the Trinity – three manifestations of one God – was a rather late invention and had not been taught by Jesus Christ. In his publications, Servet also used the Qur'ān, referring to suras that are critical of the Trinitarian dogma to support his idea of Christianity originally without the Trinity (fig. 5).

The European Qur'ān, so to say, is not only the product of numerous translations and attempts to gain more accurate insight into Islam. It is also the result of the manifold uses of the Qur'ān made by Christians in inter-Christian debates. The Qur'ān was instrumental in confirming Christian theological ideas, to contest and refute religious enemies within Christianity, and to support or undermine historical assumptions. In other words, the Qur'ān has played a pivotal role in the construction of Christian European cultural, religious, and political identities ever since the Middle Ages.

A case in point is the first print of Robert of Ketton's Latin translation of the Qur'ān in Basel in 1543. This accomplishment of the Zurich reformer Theodor Bibliander (1506–64) and the Basel printer Johannes Oporin (1507–68) was certainly a milestone in the history of Christian-European engagement with the Qur'ān. At the time, Bibliander and Oporin were confronted with considerable resistance from the Basel city council; Oporin was even in prison for a few weeks in the summer of 1542. It was only after the intervention of the Reformer Martin Luther and his public expression of support for this venture that the edition could be published.

In the following years, during the so-called age of confessionalization, the comparison of Islam and the Qur'ān became an important device in inter-Christian polemics. Protestant writers would compare Roman Catholicism with Islam, and depict the Pope and Muhammad as the two heads of the Antichrist; Roman Catholic writers, on the other hand, would refer to similarities between Islam and Protestantism – such as the focus on *Scripture*, iconoclasm etc. – as proof that they were one and the same; and both Catholic and Protestant writers would accuse Christian anti-Trinitarian movements of being followers of Muhammad.

The Qur'ān in European culture

'Works of poetry reflect the divinity of the genius ... For this reason the Qur'ān is the word of God' ('In den Werken der Dichtkunst spiegelt sich die Gottheit des Genies ... Daher ist der Coran das Wort Gottes').

These are the words of the Austrian orientalist Joseph von Hammer-Purgstall (d.1856). In some of his translations of selected verses of the Qur'ān, he tried to convey the poetic style of the Qur'ān by using rhymes and other stylistic devices. Towards the end of the eighteenth century, Europeans began to see the Qur'ān in a new light: as a masterpiece of world literature. This coincided with a broader European appreciation of Arabic, Persian, and Ottoman literature, as scholars and poets turned to the centuries-long tradition of Islamic poetry, often through their contacts with Muslim scholars. More and more European readers came to view the Qur'ān in a similar way: as a reflection of poetic genius. In the 1760s and 1770s, the Prophet Muhammad became the prototype of a poet-prophet to young writers like Johann Wolfgang von Goethe and Johann Gottfried Herder.

New translations sought to capture this genius. In the late eighteenth century, there were already attempts to convey the poetry of the Qur'ān in new European translations as part of a broader exploration of Islamic art and culture. Collectors in Europe were increasingly interested in illustrated Islamic manuscripts, including many Qur'āns, which they prized for their ornate decoration and the quality of their calligraphy. Poets like Goethe practised the Arabic script as a way to experience and appreciate Islamic culture. Drawing inspiration from Hammer's Hafiz translation, for example, Goethe's collection of orientalising poetry, the *West-Eastern Divan*, bears proof to these new attitudes.

The new approach towards the Qur'ān culminated in the work of Friedrich Rückert (d.1866). Both an accomplished orientalist and brilliant poet, Rückert devoted himself to a poetic translation of the entire Qur'ān, a work never completely finished and only published after his death but which has remained a standard translation in German ever since.

The Qur'ān in the nineteenth century

Throughout the nineteenth century, Qur'ānic studies continued to make use of looted manuscripts. However, the context of looting shifted from war times in Ottoman Europe to the European colonisation of Africa and Asia. The French and the British administered large manuscript seizures during their colonial rule. In the British Empire, looting took on an administrative form, using British

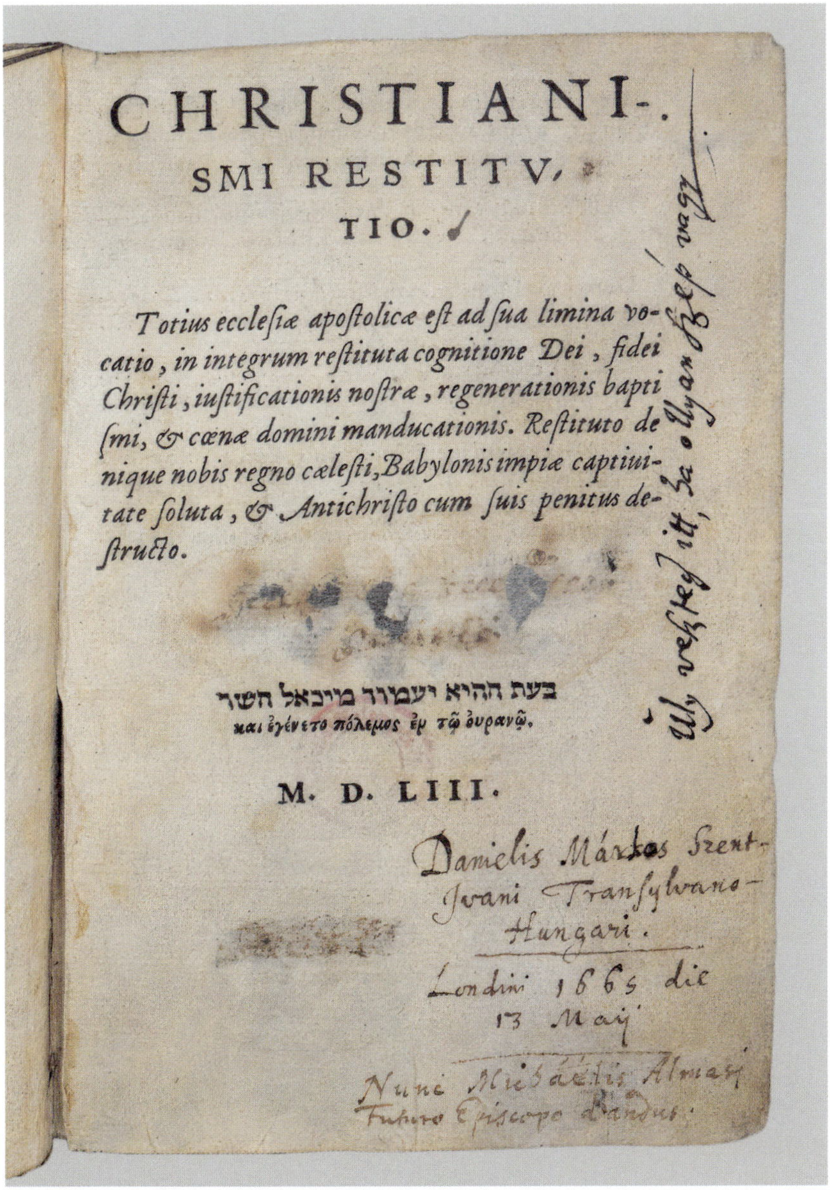

Fig. 5: Michael Servet, *Christianismi Restitutio* (Vienna, 1553). Vienna, Austrian National Library, sig. CP.4.G.2, title page

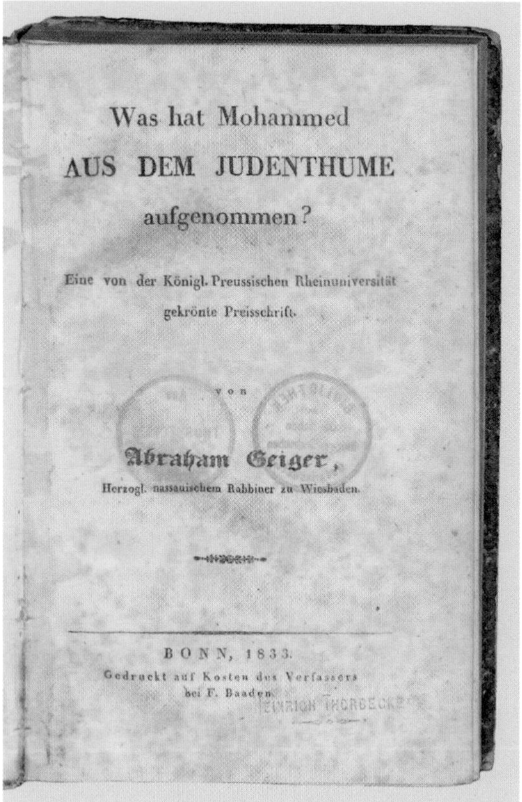

Was hat Mohammed
AUS DEM JUDENTHUME
aufgenommen?

Eine von der Königl. Preussischen Rheinuniversität
gekrönte Preisschrift.

von

Abraham Geiger,
Herzogl. nassauischem Rabbiner zu Wiesbaden.

BONN, 1833.
Gedruckt auf Kosten des Verfassers
bei F. Baaden.

Fig. 6: Abraham Geiger, *Was hat Mohammed aus dem Judenthume aufgenommen?* (Bonn, 1833), title page

prize law to mass-confiscate property, when the British East India Company assumed control of the Indian subcontinent. After the capture of Seringapatam in 1799, the British confiscated and administered 2,000 manuscripts from the library of Tipu Sultan. Claudius Buchanan, vice-provost of the College of Fort William in Calcutta, later presented an ornate Qurʾān manuscript from Tipu Sultan's library to the Archbishop of Canterbury with a dedication that frames its looting as a symbol of Christian-European superiority over the East. After the 1857 conquest of Delhi, the British confiscated more than 3,500 Arabic, Persian, and Urdu manuscripts from the Mughal Library as well as from a number of private libraries of individuals.

The French, too, in their campaign in Egypt and later during their colonial rule in Africa looted numerous collections and libraries. Several Qurʾāns were among the manuscripts taken by French troops from the encampment of the Algerian leader ʿAbd al-Qādir (Abdelkader) after the 1843 Battle of the Smala. In the nineteenth century, new scholarly disciplines like *Arabistik* (Arabic Studies), *Judaistik* (Jewish Studies) and scholarly approaches labelled *Wissenschaft des Judenthums* (Science of Judaism) und *Wissenschaft des Alten Testaments* (Science of the Old Testament) developed in Germany. In the wake of the *Haskalah* (Jewish Enlightenment), a major movement of reformation and modernisation of Judaism, European Jews portrayed Muhammad as a religious reformer and lawgiver, who could serve as a model for reforming their own religion. At the time, the first Jewish translations of the Qurʾān from Arabic were published: Rabbi Lion Ullmann translated it into German (1840); one decade later, a complete translation of the Qurʾān from Arabic to Hebrew (1857) was produced by the orientalist Hermann Reckendorf. In this prolific period, new scientific approaches to the Qurʾān emerged in Germany. In a pioneering study *Was hat Mohammed aus dem Judenthume aufgenommen* ('What did Muhammad Borrow from Judaism', 1833), Abraham Geiger demonstrated the parallels between the Qurʾān and rabbinic literature (fig. 6). Gustav Weil wrote the foundational treatise *Historisch-kritische Einleitung in den Koran* ('Historical-Critical Introduction to the Qurʾān') in 1844. The field of study culminated in the publication of Theodor Noldeke's *Geschichte des Qorans* ('History of the Qurʾān', 1860), a reference work which delves into the historical development of the Muslim Holy Scripture.

The Latin Tradition of the Qurʾān

John Tolan, University of Nantes

In medieval Europe, Christian intellectuals who read the Qurʾān generally saw it as a false revelation, a heretical scripture whose author was either Satan, Muhammad, or both. From their Christian point of view, there was no room for a prophet after Jesus Christ, no reason for a new scripture, and no legitimacy for Islam as a religion.[1] Indeed, few of them used the word 'Islam': they rather referred to the 'Law of Muhammad' or of the 'Saracens'. The first Latin scholars to read and translate the Qurʾān did so from a largely hostile point of view. Yet, their encounter with the Muslim holy book caused ambivalence: while the dominant reaction was to reject a variant 'heretical' scripture, many readers approached the Qurʾān with a mixture of hostility, curiosity, and sometimes frank admiration.

The 'Alcoran', 'Law of Mahomet', a heretical pseudo-revelation

In 1142, on the banks of the Ebro River in northeastern Spain, Abbot Peter of the rich and powerful monastery of Cluny met Robert of Ketton.[2] Robert had come from his native England ten years earlier to learn Arabic and study science. Cluny was at the head of a large monastic network, and Peter was visiting the Cluniac monasteries in Spain to ensure their respect for liturgical reform and monastic discipline. There, about 300 km from the border of the Almoravid empire, Peter conceived the idea of refuting the 'heresy of the Saracens'. To do this,

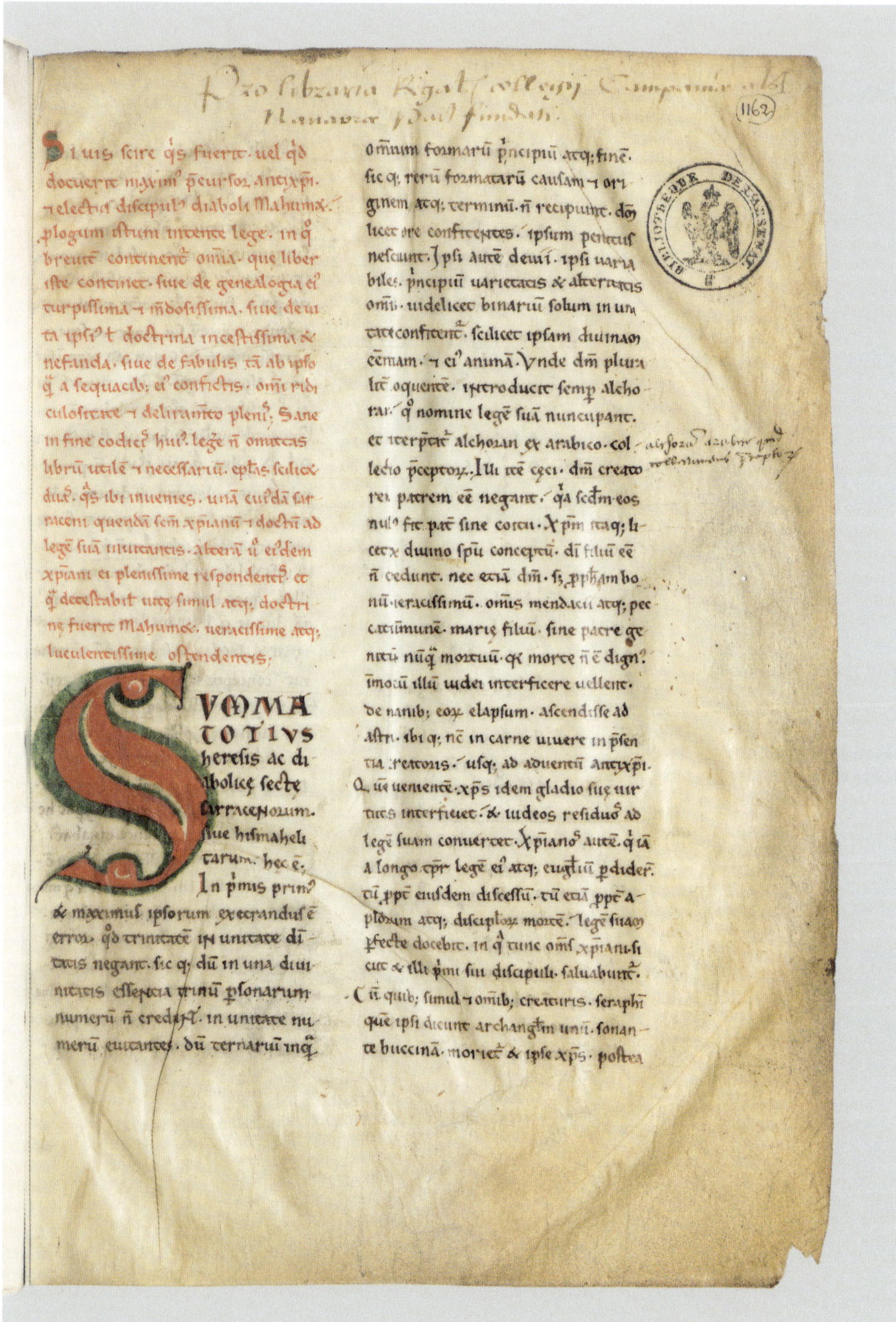

Fig. 1: Oldest manuscript of the first Latin translation of the Qurʾān by Robert of Ketton. Paris, Bibliothèque nationale de France, Ms Arsenal 1162, fol. 1r

however, he needed a translation of their holy book. As Peter explains in a letter to Abbot Bernard of Clairvaux, he met Robert 'in Spain, near the Ebro, studying the art of astrology, and I convinced him to do this work for a good price'.

Robert began to compose a Latin version of the Qur᾽ān. An arduous task, for he sought both to communicate the meaning of the holy book of Islam and to transform the rhythmic prose of the Arabic text into a 'Ciceronian' Latin worthy of a great text. Moreover, he did not just translate the Qur᾽ān, but often incorporated information from his reading of Muslim exegesis to clarify obscure passages. The result is not a literal rendering of the Muslim sacred text but a Latin adaptation, in which difficult passages are explained; it is generally impossible for the reader to distinguish between the actual text of the Qur᾽ān and the explicative material inserted by Robert. He scrupulously studied Muslim Qur᾽ānic commentaries in order to understand the standard Muslim interpretations of difficult and important passages; indeed, much of his interpolated material is adapted from works of *tafsīr*. Robert went to great lengths to provide an accurate and comprehensible Latin version of the Qur᾽ān (**fig. 1**).

Peter of Cluny's copy of Robert's translation was heavily annotated; these annotations certainly guided Peter's reading of the text. It is unclear who wrote them, although they clearly show the polemical intent of the translation. They guide the reader of the 'diabolical Qur᾽ān' by pointing out passages that would seem particularly shocking to a Christian (and especially a monastic) reader. The annotations constantly enjoin the reader to note the 'insanity', 'impiety', 'ridiculousness', 'stupidity', 'superstition', 'lying', and 'blasphemy' of what they are reading. The rubrics added at the opening of many suras make this clear: 'A stupid, vain, and impious sura', 'Sura of stupidity and lies, like the previous ones'; 'Diabolical sura, like the previous ones'. Wherever Qur᾽ānic stories differ from their Biblical counterparts, the annotator brands them as heretical or ridiculous: the Qur᾽ānic version of the Cain and Abel story is a 'stupid fable'; the story of Joseph is 'insane lies and lying insanity'. The annotator in particular attacks Muslim Christology, dubbed 'stupid and heretical sayings about Christ'. The annotations qualify Muslim traditions on Jesus and the Virgin as "monstrous and unheard-of fables'. 'Note how he everywhere says that Christ is the son of Mary, but against the Christians and the faith says that the son of Mary is not the son of God – which is the sum of all this diabolical heresy.' For the annotators, the Devil and his follower Muhammad are the authors of this heresy. Numerous annotations accuse Muhammad of being too fond of women, and of playing on the Saracens' lust by promising them *houris* in heaven. He threatens his followers with hellfire in order to get them to follow his law and to conquer Christian lands. All of this is understood in line with earlier heresies: 'Note that he everywhere promises such a paradise of carnal delights, as other heresies had done before.'

Although there were other Latin translations of the Qur'ān in later centuries, none was as successful as Robert's, of which 24 medieval manuscripts have been preserved. In these manuscripts, the text of the translation is elegantly presented: beautiful handwriting, wide margins, explanatory marginal glosses, just like manuscripts of the Bible. This showed a certain respect for the Qur'ān as the holy book of a rival religion, underlining the great ambivalence of Christian readers when approaching the Latin text of the Muslim holy book. In other words, it was a legacy of profound ambivalence that Robert of Ketton transmitted to European intellectuals who sought to understand (and often combat) Islam. His translation was one of the principal resources for Latin readers who sought to comprehend the religion of the 'Saracens' throughout the Middle Ages and beyond. In 1543, Theodore Bibliander published Robert's Qur'ān in Basel: this publication made his translation widely available to readers across Europe.

The Qur'ān translation of Mark of Toledo (1210)

Mark of Toledo, apparently unaware of Robert's translation, produced a very different Latin version of the Qur'ān in Toledo 67 years later (**fig. 2**). Mark was a deacon of the Cathedral of Toledo under Archbishop Rodrigo Jiménez de Rada (1208–47), an advisor to the Castilian kings Alfonso VIII (r. 1158–1214) and Fernando III (r. 1217–52), and a proponent of the crusade against the Almohad dynasty, which dominated al-Andalus and much of North Africa.

Archbishop Rodrigo participated in the Battle of Las Navas de Tolosa, in which Alfonso VIII and his allies routed the Almohads, initiating what Spanish historians have called the 'gran reconquista', leading to Fernando III's conquest of Cordova (1236) and Seville (1248).[3] Soon after his arrival in Toledo, Rodrigo commissioned Mark to translate the Qur'ān into Latin. Mark completed the translation in June 1210, two years before Las Navas de Tolosa, when the Almohad presence was still a serious threat.

It is in this context that Mark presents his translation as part of the intellectual and spiritual arsenal that Christians must deploy to affirm their control over their 'polluted' sanctuaries and to convert the Saracens. In the preface to his translation of the Qur'ān, Mark presents a brief, hostile biography of 'Mafometus', a skilled magician who through his travels learned the rudiments of both Judaism and Christianity, and urged his people to abandon their idolatry

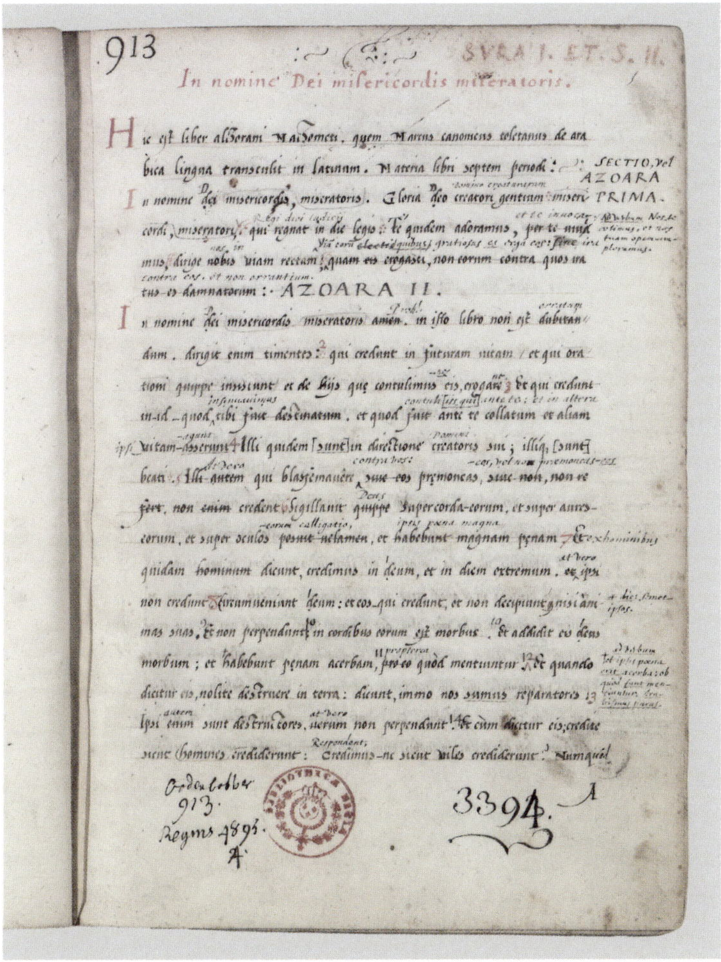

Fig. 2: Latin translation of the Qur'ān by Mark of Toledo, 1210. Paris, Bibliothèque nationale de France, Ms Lat. 3394, fol. 1r

and worship the Unique God.[4] Hesitating between Judaism and Christianity, he decided that the law of the Gospel was too difficult, as it enjoined love of one's enemy and spurning the pleasures of the flesh. Mafometus opted for Judaism yet realized that the Jews were despised everywhere because they had killed Jesus Christ. For this reason, he proclaimed that Jesus had not really been killed and promulgated a new law, the Alcoran, mixing Jewish and Christian law with his own fancy. In order to foist this law on the Arabs, he called them together outside of the city of 'Mecha' (which in Latin, Mark reminds his readers, means 'adultery'), feigned an epileptic seizure, and announced to the assembled masses that Gabriel had revealed a new law to him. Mark goes on to give a fairly accurate catalogue of Qur᾿ānic doctrine on the unity of God, the virgin birth, the role of Jesus as the prophet, the rites of prayer and ablution, fasting, and pilgrimage. Mark affirms that Mafometus established himself as a prophet and messenger of God, reigning over his people as had David and Solomon.

Having forged his new law, 'in which he speaks as one who is delirious', Mafometus 'like a magician seduced barbarous peoples through fantastic delusions'. Through war, his Saracens subdued the world, oppressing Christians from the north to the Mediterranean and from India to the west – to Spain, where 'once many priests swore holy allegiance to God, now evil men give supplication to the execrable Mafometus, and the churches which were consecrated by the hands of bishops have now become profane temples.' Mark presents the conversion of churches into mosques as an act of profanation or pollution; the reconquest of these places by Christian rulers, who will have them duly purified and reconsecrated by bishops, is implicitly legitimate.

Among those opposing the Saracens in Spain, as Mark affirms, was Archbishop Rodrigo Jiménez de Rada of Toledo. Mark describes how the good archbishop was moved to tears by seeing the Saracen oppression in his archdiocese; where priests once performed mass in honour of Christ, now the name of the 'pseudoprophet' was invoked. In the towers of the churches where bells once rang, now 'profane proclamations [the call of the muezzin] deafen the ears of the faithful.' Rodrigo, deploring this state of affairs, making his tears his arms, urged Mark to translate the book containing the Saracens' 'sacrilegious decrees and strange precepts.' The point of this translation, Mark continues, is to allow those among the orthodox who are not permitted to use arms to combat the precepts of Muslim law; in this way they can refute the 'detestable decrees' of Mafometus and in so doing, 'not a few Saracens may be dragged to the Catholic faith.' The language here is one of force and coercion. By forcibly reclaiming the Spanish churches that had been converted into mosques, Christian princes would banish the muezzin and reinstate the church bells; Christ's name, and not Mafometus's, was to be invoked. Moreover, Mark's translation of the Qur᾿ān paves the way for an intellectual combat in addition to the struggle maintained by Christian armies: knowledge of the Qur᾿ān would provide churchmen with the intellectual weaponry needed to defeat Islamic doctrine and drag the Saracens back to the faith.

It is hardly surprising that the polemical framing of Mark's Qurʾān is even more explicit than that of Robert. Yet like Robert, Mark is meticulous in his attempt to produce a version that faithfully transmits the Qurʾānic text. But where Robert incorporated material from *tafsīr* (Qurʾānic exegesis) into his translation and composed a text in high Latin style, Mark produced a more literal word by word translation, much more faithful to the word order and syntax of the original Arabic, but less comprehensible to most Latin readers, who needed the context Robert provided. Mark's spare translation was useful, above all, to those who sought to understand the original Arabic text, readers like Dominican friar Riccoldo da Montecroce.

Riccoldo da Montecroce's Arabic Qurʾān

Few medieval Latin writers engaged directly with the Arabic text of the Qurʾān. One who did was Riccoldo da Montecroce, a Dominican friar from Florence. Riccoldo travelled to Baghdad in about 1288, hoping to debate with Muslims and convert them to Christianity. He learned Arabic and read the Qurʾān, but soon realized that he would make little progress converting Muslims, who were confident that they held the 'truth' and that God had granted them victory over the Christian 'Franks': Riccoldo saw European captives brought through Baghdad and bound for slave markets after the Mamluk capture of Acre, the last mainland stronghold of the Crusader states, in 1291.[5]

Riccoldo was awed by Baghdad's wealth and beauty, distraught by the fall of Acre, and in frank admiration of the piety and learning of the Muslim scholars he met. In his *Five Letters on the Fall of Acre*, Riccoldo recounts the doubt and perplexity he experienced: Is it true, as the 'Saracens' say, that God prefers them? That Abraham, Moses, Mary, Jesus and the Apostles were all 'Saracens'? As he studied the Qurʾān, he was shocked at these ideas, which for him were blasphemies uttered by Muhammad, author of the Alcoran. What troubled him most was that such blasphemies were left unpunished. In one of his letters, he addresses the following prayer to Jesus:

> I beg you, read what he says about you, your mother, and your apostles. As you know, frequently when reading the Qurʾān in Arabic with a heart full of utter grief and impatience, I have placed the book open on your altar before your image and that of your most holy mother and said, "read, read what Mahomet says!" And it seemed to me that you did not want to read.[6]

Riccoldo filled the margins of his Arabic Qurʾān with comments and annotations: the manuscript is today in the Bibliothèque Nationale in Paris.[7] These annotations formed the basis of his subsequent anti-Qurʾānic polemic, *Contra legem sarracenorum* ('Against the Law of the Saracens'). While Riccoldo had better knowledge of the Qurʾān than any previous Latin polemicist against Islam, he presented Islam in essentially in the same way as Peter of Cluny had 150 years earlier: as the sum of all heresies. He affirmed that Christians had experienced three waves of persecution: that of the Jews and pagans in the first centuries of the Church, followed by that of the heretics. Muhammad is part of the third wave of persecutors.

> During the reign of Heraclius there arose a diabolical man, first-born of Satan, a lustful man dedicated to obscene deeds, by the name of Muhammad, who, through his [Satan's] advice and help, composed a false and nefarious law, as if from the mouth of God. He called this law Alcoran, which means anthology of the precepts of God. This Muhammad was the greatest persecutor of the Church that there ever was or shall be.[8]

Riccoldo offered a more detailed and systematic treatise on the Qurʾān than anything previously available in Latin. He outlined what he saw as its 'principal errors': the rejection of the essential Christian doctrines of the Trinity, Incarnation, Crucifixion, and Resurrection. He laboriously compared Qurʾānic doctrine to earlier Christian 'heresies', such as Nestorianism, Jacobitism, Arianism. He reproached the Qurʾān for being confusing, contradictory, unorganized, violent – in a word, *irrational*. While his Muslim interlocutors claimed that the beauty of the Qurʾān's Arabic proves its divine origins, Riccoldo affirmed the contrary: the Qurʾān is in verse, when everybody knows that God speaks to prophets clearly, *in prose*. The real author of the Alcoran, Riccoldo affirmed, is the Devil. When Emperor Heraclius defeated the Persians and destroyed their golden and silver idols, the Devil realized he could no longer defend polytheism; nor could he fight the growing recognition of the Old and New Testament. Instead, he decided to create a new law, composed of elements from both Mosaic and Gospel laws, in order to lead the world astray. And Satan found his man: 'a certain diabolical man by the name of Mahomet, idolatrous in religion, impoverished of any fortune, arrogant in spirit and a very famous sorcerer.'

Despite Riccoldo's knowledge of the Qurʾān and familiarity with Muslim scholars, he fell back on the hostile legends fabricated by earlier Christian polemicists. 'Mahomet composed a sort of law, taking from his associates some elements of the Old Testament and some of the New Testament, but the people did not yet have the Alcoran.' Indeed, Riccoldo wrote, when Muhammad died the text of the Alcoran had not yet been established, and this subsequently became a cause of disagreement and conflict. From his reading of Qur'ānic commentaries and his discussions with Muslim intellectuals in Baghdad, he had become acquainted with different versions of how the Qur'ān was composed after Muhammad's death. Here he used these stories to attempt to discredit the Muslim holy book. In other words, despite his knowledge of Arabic and Islam, and his friendly intellectual exchanges with Muslims in Baghdad, he retained the perspective of a Dominican missionary and saw the Qur'ān as heretical. His learned assault on the Qur'ān would prove very influential on European authors over the following centuries. For these Latin Christians of the twelfth to fourteenth centuries, Robert of Ketton, Peter of Cluny, Riccoldo da Montecroce and others, the Qur'ān was a heretical pseudo-revelation, opposed to Christian truth.

The Council of Basel and new ways of reading the Qur'ān in fifteenth-century Europe

The years from 1451 to 1461 saw a significant number of texts about Islam and the 'Turkish menace' as, in reaction to the Ottoman siege and capture (in 1453) of Constantinople, European Christians debated the merits of crusade and mission; a number of these texts were written by ecclesiastics who had met at the Council of Basel (1431–37) and Ferrara/Florence (1438–45). They all agreed on the urgency of the issue, but differed both in their assessment of the problem and the solutions they proposed. Their views on these topics were coloured by their preoccupations during the councils, which strove for the unity of Christendom by attempting to put an end to the papal schism and to reconcile the Catholic Church and various eastern Churches: Christian unity was all the more necessary in face of the Ottoman threat. This context of a Latin Europe threatened by Ottoman expansion in many ways reinforced negative perceptions of Islam and the Qur'ān as heretical deviations of the 'True Religion'. Paradoxically, however, the same context also provoked new studies of the Qur'ān as well as more creative and sympathetic readings of the Muslim holy book.[9]

After meeting in Basel, two friends began to study the Qur'ān: Nicholas of Cusa and Juan de Segovia. Twenty years after their first encounter, Nicholas wrote his *De Pace Fidei* ('On the Peace of Faith', 1453), a fictitious dialogue in which representatives of different religious traditions discuss faith. Nicholas emphasized the unity of belief and purpose among the sages. Their 'faith and religion are one, under a diversity of rites' (*una religio in rituum varietate*), and the capacity to understand this unity and respect the diversity has the potential to lead to a greater understanding of God and the achievement of peace among people of different religions. In this irenic dialogue, Muhammad is mentioned only once, in very neutral terms, as one whom the Arabs believe has transmitted divine commandments. Dialogue between representatives of different faiths can lead to unity, Nicholas affirms. Peaceful discussion may lead the way to unity of faith among a diversity of practice not only among Christians (Eastern and Western), but also with Muslims.[10]

Juan de Segovia also promoted peaceful dialogue as the appropriate response to Islam. Juan was in the Savoyard monastery of Aiton when he received word of the fall of Constantinople in 1453. In 1453–54, he wrote to both Nicholas of Cusa and Bishop Jean Germain of Chalons, suggesting a scheme of organized debates between Christian and Muslim intellectuals to rationally persuade the latter of the truth of Christianity. Nicholas responded warmly to the idea; Jean Germain was sceptical; he promoted a new crusade against the Ottomans. Juan's idea (to which he frequently alluded in his different letters) was to send a delegation of Christian leaders to speak with Muslim leaders about the faith: he never specified exactly who should be involved. The goal was to respond with peaceful Christian dialogue instead of violence, and to dispel Muslims' misconceptions about Christianity (that the Trinity contradicts monotheism, for example). This conciliar strategy, which had sought solutions to conflicts with heretics (Hussites) and schismatics (Eastern Christians), could, Juan de Segovia hoped, bring peace between Muslims and Christians in the short term, and Muslims' conversion to Christianity in the long term.[11]

Juan sought to engage with Islam, its beliefs and texts: his strategy was very different from that of Cusa's *De Pace Fidei*. He wanted to study the Qur᾽ān, yet he was unsatisfied with Robert of Ketton's Latin translation. In 1455, he convinced the *faqīh* of his native Segovia, 'Īsā ibn Jābir, to come to Aiton for four months and help him produce a new translation. Juan describes how 'Īsā copied the Arabic text of the Qur᾽ān in one column, then composed a Castilian translation in a parallel column. 'Īsā became Juan's teacher of Arabic, as they studied the text together and discussed its interpretation and translation. 'Īsā then returned to Segovia, and Juan wrote in a third column his own Latin translation from the Spanish.[12] At the same time he was working with 'Īsā on the Qur'ān, he also composed his own tract on how to argue against Muslims, *De gladio divini Spiritus in corda mittendo Sarracenorum* ('On Thrusting the Sword of the Holy Spirit into the Hearts of the Saracens'). The violence in the title is metaphorical: it is not the sword of steel, which Muhammad and his followers wield, that will give victory to Christians, but the sword of the Holy Spirit, which is to say, the word of God. Indeed, Juan's opposition to crusade is based to no small extent on the opposition between Christ's message and method and those of Muhammad.

Nicholas of Cusa was familiar with the anti-Muslim polemics of Peter of Cluny, Riccoldo da Montecroce and others. In 1461, he proposed something quite different, a 'Sifting of the Qur'ān' (*Cribratio Alcorani*), in order to identify nuggets of truth and wisdom. His approach is essentially positive; he differs from many of his predecessors and contemporaries in his efforts to find a *pia interpretatio* ('pious interpretation') of the prophet's intentions and of Muslim doctrines and practices. Nicholas judges that, where the Qur'ān differs from the Bible, it was the result of Muhammad's ignorance of Christ, not his hostility. He concludes that the Qur'ān's rejection of the Trinity is best understood as a refusal of polytheism and idolatry; Muhammad did not teach the crucifixion and resurrection of Christ because he felt it would compromise his attempts to lead idolatrous Arabs to strict monotheism. In other words, Muhammad, understanding the truth, revealed only as much of it as he felt would be effective in abolishing idolatry and establishing monotheism.

In a similar way, Nicholas gives pious interpretations of other Qur'ānic passages that contradict Christian doctrine. If Muhammad denies that Christ died crucified, it is because he wishes to glorify Him in the eyes of uncultured Arabs who would see death by crucifixion as shameful. Nicholas also excused Muhammad for promising sensual delights in heaven, arguing that such descriptions are to be understood metaphorically, and that the wise among the Saracens indeed do so. On these key points, Nicholas stresses Muhammad's good intentions, affirming that he was doing what he thought was necessary to bring the Arabs away from idolatry and to monotheism.

Nicholas is in this way the first Latin Christian author to see the prophet's life and mission as positive. This is not to say that he shows no hostility towards Muhammad. On the contrary, he sees the errors of the Qur'ān as the product of the influence of Muhammad's frequenting Jews and Nestorian Christians, and accuses him of pandering to his own lust and ambition: 'Muhammad sought not the glory of God and the salvation of men but rather his own glory'. Yet we see for the first time a Latin Christian author recognizing in the Muslim prophet not merely a divine scourge sent to punish Christians, but a partially (if imperfectly) inspired leader whom God used to spread monotheism and abolish idolatry.

Nicholas attempts to establish a true faith that transcends confessional and ritual differences, a universal truth to which sages of all religions can agree. But of course his vision is profoundly Christian: the Qurʾān and other rival scriptures can be true only in as far as they confirm the truth of Christianity. Nicholas' novel approach to the Qurʾān provoked interest among European scholars, as we see from the testimony of the five extant fifteenth-century manuscripts of the *Cribratio* and five printed editions between 1488 and 1565. In particular, his work is printed in 1543 by Theodor Bibliander alongside Robert of Ketton's Latin Qurʾān, Riccoldo da Montecroce's anti-Qurʾānic polemic, and other texts on Islam, comprising a publication which became one of the most important Latin humanist volumes on Islam.

The work of Nicholas and many of the medieval authors we have examined here became essential tools for sixteenth-century authors who wrote about Islam in the context of the Ottoman expansion into Europe and the wars of religion between Catholics and Protestants. The legacy of these medieval European intellectuals had a profound impact on how European Christians viewed the Qurʾān and Islam over centuries to come.

1 John Tolan, *Saracens: Islam in the Medieval European Imagination* (New York, 2002).

2 On Robert's translation, see Thomas Burman, *Reading the Qur'ān in Latin Christendom, 1140–1560* (Philadelphia, 2009); Oscar De la Cruz and Cándida Ferrero Hernández, 'Robert of Ketton', in David Thomas et al. (eds.), *Bibliographical History of Christian-Muslim Relations*, vol. 2 (Leiden, 2011; hereafter CMR), 508–19; Tristan Vigliano, 'Le Coran des Latins: un impossible décentrement ? Les deux cas exemplaires de Robert de Ketton et Jean de Ségovie', *Réforme, Humanisme, Renaissance* 78 (2014), 137–74; Cándida Ferrero Hernández and John Tolan (eds.), *The Latin Qur'ān, 1143–1500: Translation, Transition, Interpretation* (Berlin, 2021).

3 Matthias Maser, 'Rodrigo Jiménez de Rada," in CMR 4:343–55; Maser, *Die Historia Arabum des Rodrigo Jimenez de Rada: Arabische Traditionen und die Identität der Hispania im 13. Jahrhundert* (Berlin, 2006); Lucy Pick, *Conflict and Coexistence: Archbishop Rodrigo and the Muslims and Jews in Medieval Spain* (Ann Arbor, 2004).

4 Nàdia Petrus Pons (ed.), *Alchoranus latinus, quem transtulit Marcus canonicus Toletanu* (Madrid, 2016).

5 Rita George-Tvrtkovic, *A Christian Pilgrim in Medieval Iraq: Riccoldo da Montecroce's Encounter with Islam* (Turnhoult, 2012); Thomas E. Burman, 'Riccoldo da Monte di Croce', in CMR 4; Riccoldo da Monte Croce, *Tractatus seu disputatio contra Saracenos et Alchoranum*, edited, translated, and commented by Daniel Pachurka (Wiesbaden, 2016).

6 George-Tvrtkovic 2012 (see note 5), 163.

7 José Martínez Gázquez and François Déroche, 'Lire et traduire le Coran au Moyen Âge. Les gloses latines du manuscrit arabe 384 de la BnF', *Comptes-rendus des séances de l'année – Académie des inscriptions et belles-lettres* 154 (2010), 1021–40.

8 Riccoldo da Montecroce, *Contra Sectam Sarracenorum*, prologue, http://www.e-theca.net/emiliopanella/riccoldo2/cls001.htm (accessed 17 July 2024).

9 Jacob Langeloh, *Der Islam auf dem Konzil von Basel (1431–1449)* (Wiesbaden, 2019).

10 Nicholas of Cusa, *Nicholas of Cusa's De pace fidei and Cribratio Alkorani: translation and analysis*, trans. Jasper Hopkins (Minneapolis, 1990); Ian Christopher Levy, Rita George-Tvrtkovic, and Donald Duclow (eds.), *Nicholas of Cusa and Islam Polemic and Dialogue in the Late Middle Ages* (Leiden, 2014); John Tolan, 'Nicholas of Cusa,' in CMR 5; Tristan Vigliano, *Parler aux musulmans: quatre intellectuels face à l'Islam à l'orée de la Renaissance* (Genève: 2016), 139–207.

11 Davide Scotto, *Juan de Segovia e il Corano: convertire i musulmani nell'Europa del Quattrocento* (Loveno di Menaggio, 2022); *Anne Marie Wolf, Juan de Segovia and the Fight for Peace: Christians and Muslims in the Fifteenth Century* (Notre Dame, 2014), 129–74; Vigliano 2016 (see note 10), 209–303.

12 Thomas Burman, *Reading the Qur'ān in Latin Christendom*, 178–88; Wolf 2014 (see note 11), 188–92; Gerard Wiegers, 'Içe de Gebir,' in CMR 5; José Martínez Gázquez, 'El Prólogo de Juan de Segobia al Corán (Qur'ān) trilingüe (1456),' *Mittellateinisches Jahrbuch* 38 (2003); Davide Scotto, 'De pe a pa': Il Corano trilingue di Juan de Segovia (1456) e la conversione pacifica dei musulmani,' *Rivista di Storia e Letteratura Religiosa* 48 (2012); Ana Echevarria, *The Fortress of Faith: the Attitude towards Muslims in Fifteenth-Century Spain* (Leiden, 1999).

Muslim Minorities in Iberia and Central Europe

Mercedes García-Arenal, Spanish National Research Council
Katarzyna K. Starczewska, Spanish National Research Council

European Muslims before the Ottoman era

Historical Muslim communities in Europe, other than those resulting from Ottoman expansion, were primarily found in two regions: the Iberian Peninsula, home to the *Mudejars* (Muslims remaining after the Christian reconquest) and *Moriscos* (former Muslims forced to convert to Christianity), and the Grand Duchy of Lithuania (GDL), home to the *Tatars* (Muslims settled in the Polish-Lithuanian Commonwealth). Finding themselves surrounded by predominantly Christian societies, these groups developed remarkably similar strategies for preserving their religious culture and knowledge.

The settlements of these European Muslim communities emerged independently from and prior to the Ottoman expansion into Europe. Over a span of almost two centuries in the case of the Morisco population (from the conquest of Granada in 1492 to the expulsion of the Moriscos in 1609), and three centuries in the case of the GDL Tatars (from the seventeenth to the nineteenth century), their literary production was exclusively handwritten. Numerous members of both groups preserved their Muslim piety, but many were unfamiliar with Arabic, the holy language of Qurʾānic revelation. Without access to one another's culture, both the Moriscos and the GDL Tatars adapted the Arabic alphabet to write in their vehicular languages, namely Romance and Slavic respectively. This adaptation strategy enabled them to maintain the sacred aspect of their writings while translating the Qurʾān into a language they fully understood. Despite these striking similarities, there were also notable differences. The GDL Tatars were granted full religious freedom, while the Moriscos were heavily persecuted for any signs of adherence to Islam. Nonetheless, both groups left behind considerable corpora of religious manuscripts, some of which we present in this exhibition.

Muslim communities in Iberia: between religious confrontation and knowledge transfer

Thanks to the long presence of Muslims in Iberia – both as inhabitants of Islamic territories (al-Andalus and the Nasrid Kingdom of Granada) and as Muslim minorities in the Christian kingdoms – the Iberian Peninsula provides fertile ground for studying the cultural history of the Qurʾān in Europe. From the mid-twelfth to at least the end of the seventeenth century in Iberia, Muslim religious scholars and scribes on the one hand, and Christian scholars and converts to Christianity on the other, endeavoured to copy, transmit, interpret, and translate the Qurʾān. Their efforts are essential for understanding the significance of the Qurʾān in Europe. It was in Iberia that the pioneering Latin translations of the Qurʾān by Robert of Ketton and Mark of Toledo were made in the twelfth and thirteenth centuries. Our focus, however, will be on the agency of Iberian Muslims.

Throughout the Middle Ages and during the long process known as the 'Reconquest', the northern Christian kingdoms of Spain slowly expanded their frontiers southwards. In consequence, large minorities of Muslims, the so-called Mudejars, found themselves living in Christian territories, where they were allowed to preserve and practice their faith under certain conditions. This marked the first time in history that significant numbers of Muslims came to live under non-Muslim rule.

These Muslims in the Christian kingdoms interpreted and translated their sacred scripture for their own use, as they grew increasingly familiar with the Romance vernaculars and gradually lost their knowledge of Arabic. There were translations from Arabic to vernacular Castilian or Aragonese, written in the Latin alphabet or more frequently in what is called *Aljamiado*, a Romance vernacular in Arabic script. The first written evidence of such translations appears in Aragon, dated 1415.

Nevertheless, collaboration certainly existed across religious borders: in Castile, we have the famous example of the translation of the Qurʾān by Juan de Segovia in collaboration of a Muslim jurist learned in Islamic law, ʿĪsā ibn Jābir (in Castilian known as Içe de Gebir), in 1456. ʿĪsā was a Mudejar who never converted to Christianity. This translation has not been found, but we know of it through its Latin preface by Segovia and his correspondence. Juan de Segovia and ʿĪsā ibn Jābir had different aims: while the former wanted to translate the Qurʾān as an aid in converting Muslims, ʿĪsā wanted to translate it to better educate the Muslim population of Castile.

A decade after the capitulation of Granada in 1492 and the conquest of the Nasrid Kingdom (also known as the Emirate of Granada, the last independent Muslim state in western Europe), the so-called Catholic Monarchs, Ferdinand and Isabella, banned Islam from all of Castile in 1502. If the Muslim population wanted to avoid expulsion from the crown territories, they had to convert to Christianity. Under the Crown of Aragon, however, Muslims could still practice Islam until 1526, when they too were forced to convert to Christianity or face expulsion. The converted Iberian Muslims were called Moriscos.

The forced conversion of Muslims to Christianity was completed by the 1520s; those who wanted to remain Muslim had to practice their religion secretly and, from the 1530s onward, under persecution by the Inquisition. Having been baptised as Christians, they could be charged with 'apostasy' if they were found practising Islam. Even though King Philip II had issued an edict for the Kingdom of Granada in 1567, which banned the oral and written use of the Arabic language, Arabic was still spoken and written in parts of Spain by the population of Islamic origin. Inquisition files contain detailed information on the use of Arabic up to the general expulsion of the Moriscos in 1609–14.

This historical background shows why Iberia offers a unique case study for the history of the Qurʾān in Europe. On the one hand, no other area in western Europe experienced such an intense and enduring confrontation with Islam; on the other, no other area had such a close and productive entanglement with Islam and Muslims. This long process began in the twelfth century with the first translations of the Qurʾān into Latin. The most important period of translation, however, was in the sixteenth century. It was a time and context when Arabic books and Arabic speakers familiar with the Qurʾān and its exegesis coexisted with Christian populations, often occupying the same spaces, centres of power, and (religious) education as Christian scholars. In Christian Iberia, the proximity of Islamic traditions and sources, and the availability of informants (mostly, but not exclusively, converts) offered Christians with an interest in the Qurʾān privileged access to Islam. This resulted in a conceptual Christianization of Islam (even in anti-Islamic texts), often based on the lived experience of Muslims, and entailed an understanding of Islam that was not limited to the Qurʾān but more attuned to the religious significance of Qurʾānic interpretation (*tafsīr*) and Islamic tradition (*ḥadīṯ*). The collaboration and contact between members of both religions also produced a certain need for separation and gave rise to sentiments of rejection on both sides. The communities were engaged in drawing clear boundaries that distinguished them from one another. Iberia, therefore, serves as a laboratory for studying the construction, destruction, and blurring of religious, cultural, and political identities.

Material testimonies of religious adherence

There were Arabic Qurʾāns copied by Muslims throughout the Morisco period up to the beginning of the seventeenth century; some of these are rich and well-decorated manuscripts that reveal the patronage of wealthy Muslim families and the existence of copyists, calligraphers, and illustrators, including access to quality paper and ink (fig. 1).

A notable example of this wealth is a Qurʾān preserved in Madrid at the Real Academia de la Historia, copied in 1597 by Muḥammad b. Muḥammad Ballester in Aranda de Moncayo (Aragon). Although relatively few of these manuscripts survived, we know from Inquisition trials that they existed in large numbers but were often confiscated and burned by the Inquisition or taken abroad by the Moriscos when they were expelled in 1609–1614. Many were found after the expulsion, hidden in walls or under roofs in houses that had belonged to Moriscos. The last of these finds took place in 2003 in the wall of a house in the village of Cútar (Málaga), where a wonderful Qurʾān was found together with other Arabic books and documents. The so-called *Cútar Qurʾān* was probably copied in the late twelfth or early thirteenth century; the date makes this Qurʾān exceptional, as most surviving copies of Mudejar and Morisco Qurʾāns date from the sixteenth century (fig. 2).

For Muslims, the act of translating the Qurʾān was not straightforward, and Mudejars had to consult Muslim authorities to determine if it was a legitimate endeavour. A decade before the forced conversion of the Aragonese Muslims to Christianity, for example, the office of the four chief judges (*qāḍīs*) of Mamluk Cairo issued responses at the request of Mudejars from Aragon. One of the questions the Mudejars addressed to the judges was whether it was legitimate to translate the Qurʾān into non-Arabic languages. All the jurists agreed on the legitimacy of vernacular Qurʾānic explications; in other words, a translation in

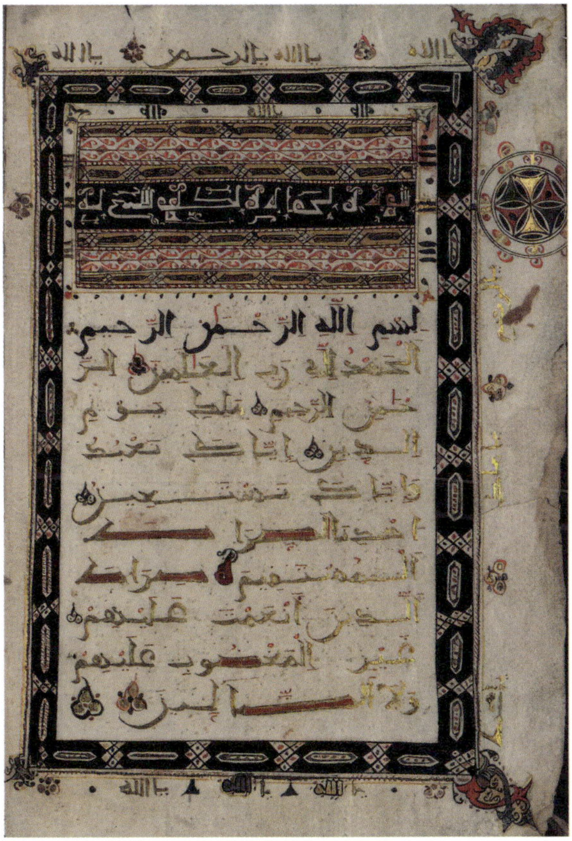

Fig. 1: Qurʾān copied in Aranda de Moncayo, 1597. Madrid, Biblioteca de la Real Academia de la Historia, Ms 11/10619 (olim Codera 288), fol. 2v

the sense of providing a commentary (*tafsīr*) was approved. In fact, legal rulings (*fatwas*) generally tried to support the religious life of Muslim minorities, but they aimed to limit the use of literal Qurʾān translations and of the Romance vernacular in religious affairs.

Remarkably, only one complete Qurʾān translation from the Mudejar–Morisco period has survived. The so-called *Toledo Qurʾān* was copied in 1606 in Castilian language and Latin script from an exemplar written in Aljamiado (**fig. 3**). More common are the 'abridged' or abbreviated Qurʾāns, of which nearly fifty examples exist, in both Arabic and Aljamiado. These consisted of a selection of

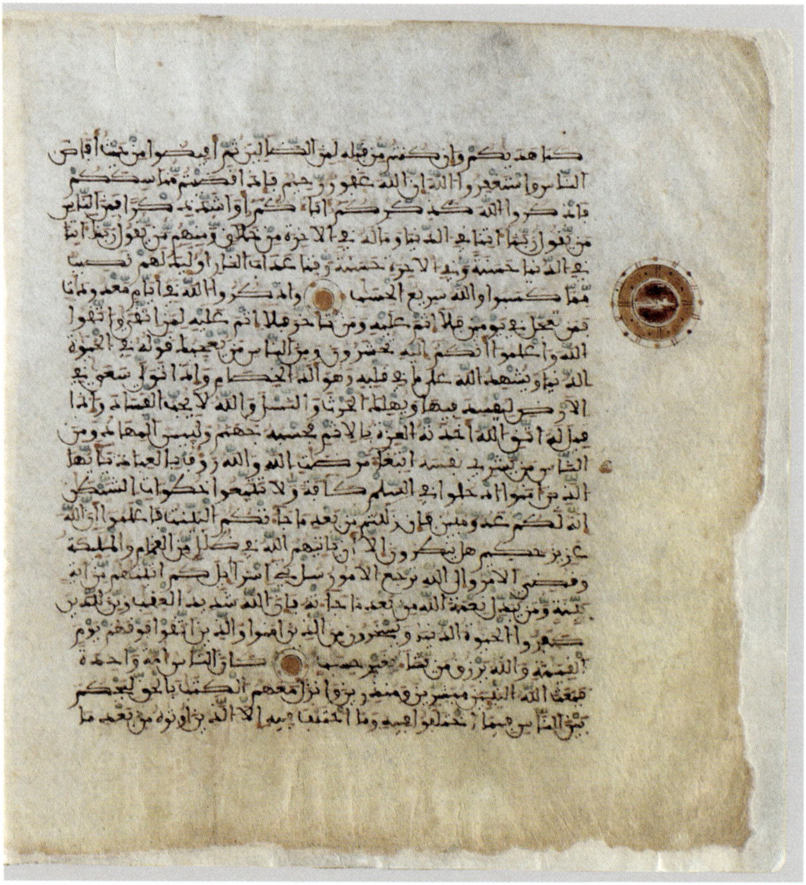

Fig. 2: *Corán de Cútar* (c.13th cent.).
Málaga, Archivo Histórico Provincial, Ms L-14028, fol. 7v

the chapters and verses most recited in daily prayer, generally arranged by the length of the suras, with the longest suras placed first (**fig. 4**).

The abridged Qurʾāns demonstrate the agency of Moriscos concerning the Qurʾānic text. They provide prayers, especially funerary prayers, selected to counteract the fact that Moriscos were living in a Christian society, were forced to practice their religion clandestinely, and were obliged to comply with Christian rituals. For this reason, these 'abridged Qurʾāns' served as strongholds of Muslim identity.

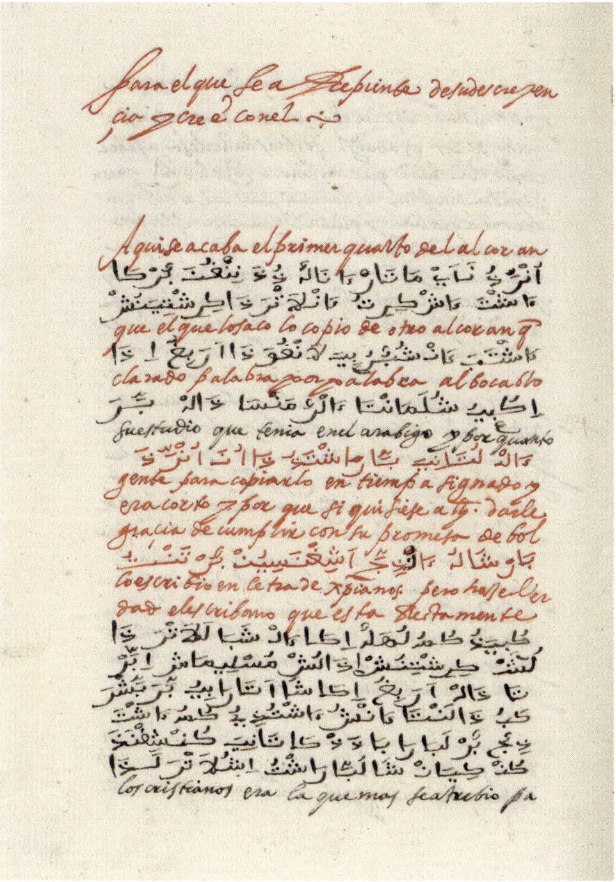

Fig. 3: *Coran de Toledo*, 1606. Toledo, Biblioteca de Castilla-La Mancha, Ms 235, fol. 81v

There is another type of abridged Qurʾān in Arabic but organized in reverse order, starting with the last suras and continuing in the opposite order of the Book. These Qurʾāns seem to have been used as an aid for memorizing the Qurʾān. Inquisition trials show the importance of memory and orality for Moriscos, to the point that some of them preferred to use wooden tablets for memorization instead of paper, as the former could be washed or erased.

An important convert from Islam with great influence on the reception of the Qurʾān in the early modern period was Juan Andrés, allegedly the son of a

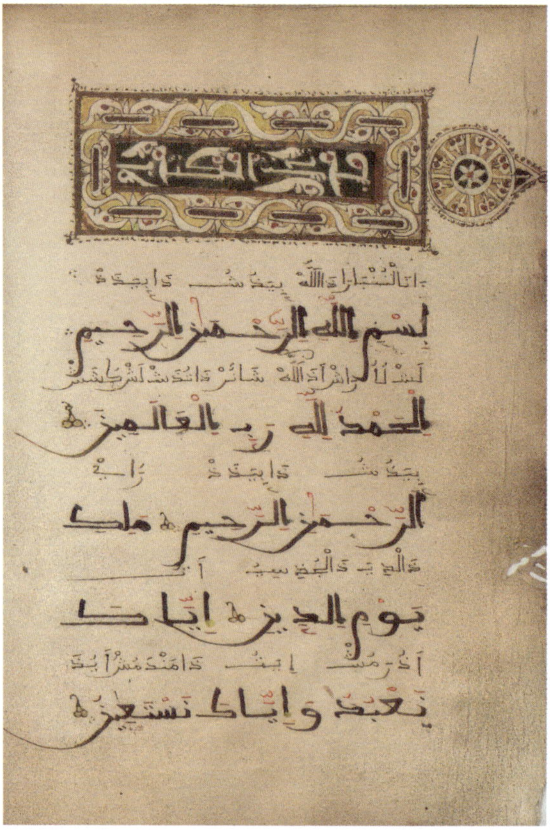

Fig. 4: Qurʾān, bilingual interlinear, 16th cent.
Madrid, CSIC Biblioteca Tomás Navarro Tomás, Ms RESC/25, fol. 1v

jurist and a community leader (*alfaqui*) from Xàtiva, who converted to Christianity in 1487. In 1515, he authored an anti-Islamic polemic entitled *Confusión o confutación de la secta Mahomética y del Alcorán* ('Confusion or Confutation of the Muhammadan Sect and of the Qurʾān'), which contains numerous passages from the Qurʾān, copied both in transliterated phonological Arabic (in Latin script) and in translation. The work is among the earliest datable examples of the Qurʾān in Romance translation to have survived. Juan Andrés's book was translated into Italian in 1537 and then from Italian into various European languages, becoming one of the most widely circulated sources of knowledge of Islam until the eighteenth century.

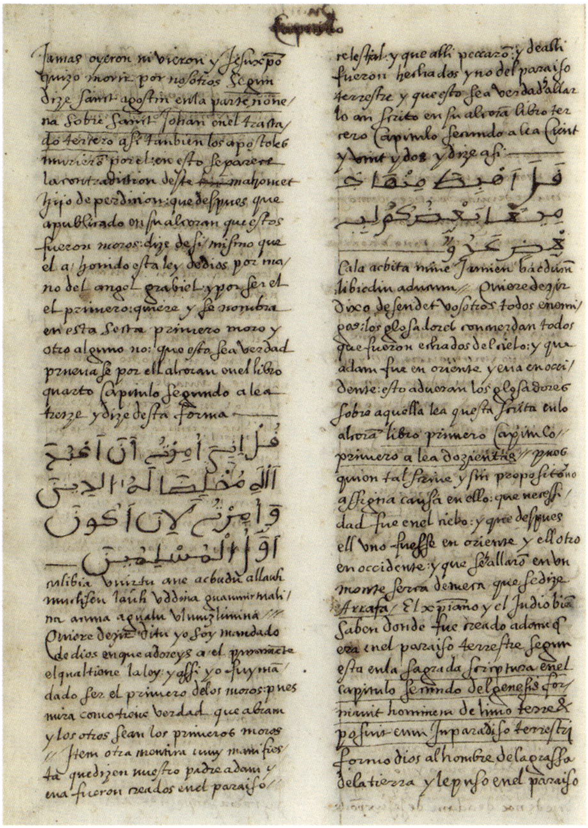

Fig. 5: Joan Martí Figuerola, *Lumbre de fe contra el Alcorán*, 1521.
Madrid, Biblioteca de la Real Academia de la Historia, Ms 19-36, fol. 12v

Six years after Juan Andrés's *Confusión*, but before the Aragonese decree of conversion, Joan Martí de Figuerola, a priest from a nearby region of Valencia, finished his *Lumbre de fe contra el Alcorán* ('Fire/Light of Faith against the Qurʾān'). This work presents a similar exposition against the Qurʾān, including hundreds of Qurʾānic passages. Martí de Figuerola quotes the Qurʾān in Arabic by means of phonological transcription and provides Spanish translations, referring to historical religious authorities to explain each passage (**fig. 5**).

Figuerola also includes illustrations along with the Arabic text of the quotations he writes out in Arabic script. Martí de Figuerola did not use Juan Andrés's translation but instead relied on sources from Islamic tradition provided by

Juan Gabriel, a recently converted religious savant from Teruel, who translated parts of the Qurʾān and accompanied him on his conversion campaigns.

The efforts of Martí de Figuerola and other authors of these polemical treatises that relied heavily on Qurʾānic sources need to be connected with Egidio da Viterbo's Latin translation, which is unfortunately now lost. What we have is a copy of the original (which was originally found at the Royal Library at El Escorial and was later lost, probably in the fire of 1671); it was made in 1621 by the Scottish orientalist David Colville, who worked in that library for many years. Colville's manuscript contains a translation of the Qurʾān into Latin, which had been commissioned by an Italian cardinal from a scholar of Spanish Muslim origin who lived in the Iberian Peninsula. The same text was then edited and reworked by another convert from Islam to Christianity, al-Hassan ibn Muhammad al-Wassan, also known by his adopted Christian name 'Leo Africanus', of Muslim Iberian (Granadan) stock, who lived in Italy. Also connected to Egidio's version is the *Corán de Bellús* (**fig. 6**).

Bellús is a village near Valencia where the manuscript was copied in 1518, precisely when Egidio was in Spain. The manuscript contains interlinear translations and glosses in Latin, Castilian, and Catalan, which proves that the *Bellús Qurʾān* landed in the hands of Christian scholars who used it as a tool for studying Islam's sacred book. This makes the *Bellús Qurʾān* another important witness to the process of collective and individual study of the text of the Qurʾān: it preserves traces of all the phases and figures involved in this process, from the initial work of the Muslim scribe who produced a careful, professional copy to the insertion of explanatory glosses in the margins and the marking up of parts of text that were considered of interest and would later be used in sermons and different works with the goal of converting Muslims.

The stories of Egidio and many others before him (from Robert of Ketton to Juan de Segovia) show that collaboration with Muslim scholars or Muslim converts was fundamental to the enterprise of Christian evangelization and anti-Islamic polemic in Iberia. For instance, Juan Andrés was a convert, and Bernardo Pérez de Chinchón, who wrote *Antialcorano* around 1528, worked on the Qurʾān with Islamic intellectuals and religious authorities in Valencia: with the judge of Valencia (whom he calls Moscayre or Mangay) and the scholar Zumilla (José Arábigo). Martí de Figuerola collaborated with the converted imam of Teruel. All evidence indicates that the authors of anti-Muslim polemics considered these learned men as the best intermediaries to convert their communities, and the ones most amenable to following and

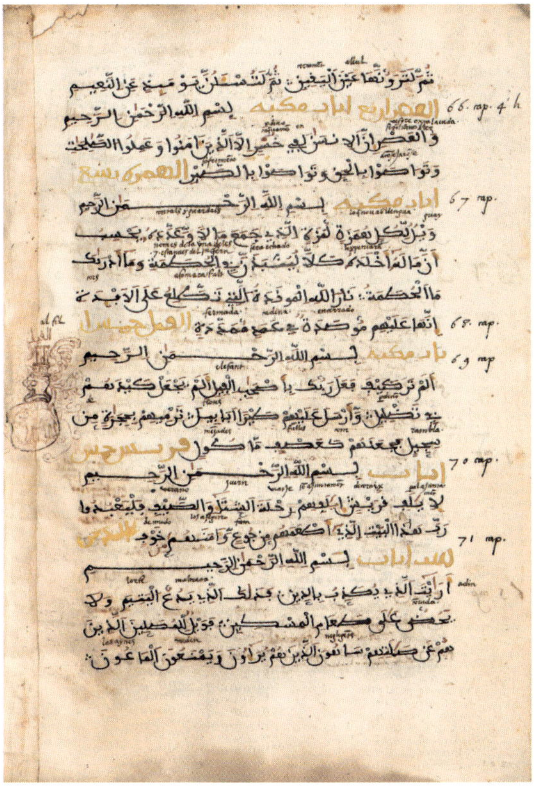

Fig. 6: *Corán de Bellús*, 1518.
Munich, Bayerische Staatsbibliothek, Cod. arab 7, fol. 200v

understanding the theological messages contained in this literary genre of religious controversy.

The different types of Qurʾān translations made in sixteenth-century Spain show how different registers of discourse could be employed for different audiences. In approaching these texts, we should think in clusters of people or networks of circulation of individual texts, and contexts in which these texts were then assigned meaning.

Muslims in the Polish-Lithuanian Commonwealth

The Polish-Lithuanian Commonwealth as a political entity was officially established in July 1569. Nevertheless, it had effectively acted as a united territory since

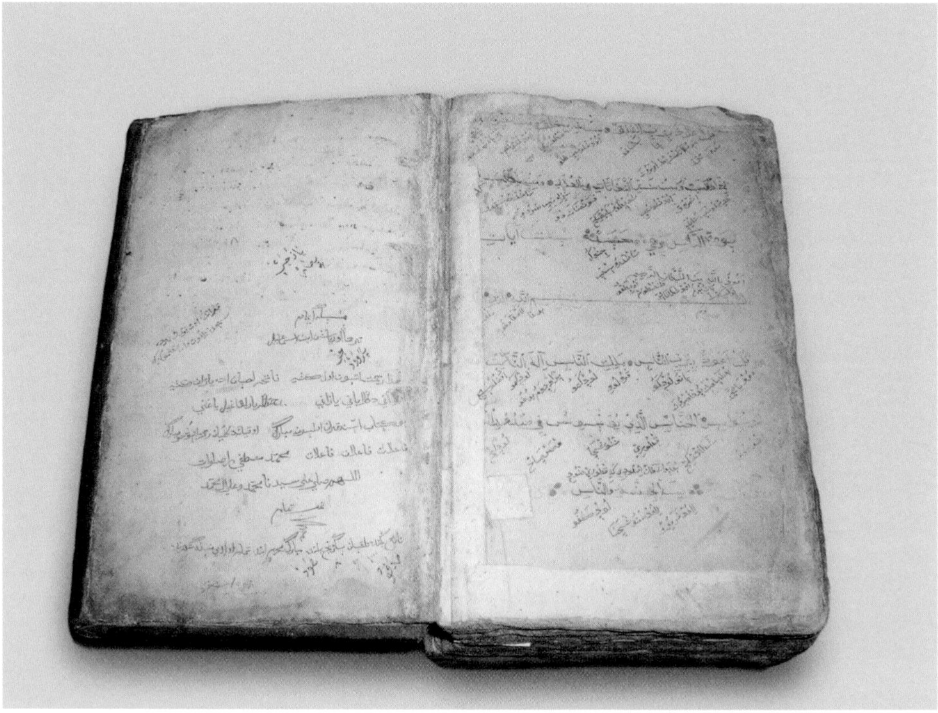

Fig. 7: Minsk *Tefsir*. Yakub Kolas Central Scientific Library of the National Academy of Sciences of Belarus, P16–18/Sr2 (R214), fols. 513v-514r

1386, thanks to the marriage of the monarch of the Kingdom of Poland, Jadwiga (Hedwig), and the head of the Grand Duchy of Lithuania, Grand Duke Jogaila; the latter was crowned, upon his conversion from paganism to Christianity, as King Władysław II Jagiełło of Poland.

The eighteenth-century partitions (territorial seizures and annexations, dividing up the lands of the Commonwealth among the Habsburg monarchy, the Kingdom of Prussia, and the Russian Empire) put an end to this vast and populous European country. The First Partition (1772) and the Second Partition (1793) greatly reduced the state's size, and the Third Partition (1795) eliminated the Commonwealth altogether.

Before these partitions, the Polish-Lithuanian Commonwealth proved to be a successful realization of the concept of a common state for ethnically, linguistically, and confessionally distinct communities for several centuries. The state system of this federal 'republican monarchy' was based on civil rights, allowing each different community to recognize the state as its own. Moreover, it attracted many religious-political refugees from other European states. We might even argue that religious freedom was always seen as an intrinsic component of the Polish-Lithuanian Commonwealth's domestic policy. Accommodating one of the greatest Jewish diasporas of the sixteenth century, native Muslim communities (the Tatars of the GDL), Turkic-speaking adherents of a branch of Judaism based on the original meaning of Torah (Kipchak Karaites), and numerous groups of non-Catholic Christians (including the Oriental Armenian Church and the Protestant anti-Trinitarian movement), the Commonwealth was a stronghold of religious freedom in a period when religious persecution was the norm throughout the rest of Europe.

The process of Tatar settlement in the GDL can be divided into two phases. In the first stage in the fourteenth and fifteenth centuries, the migration of Tatars from the empire of the Golden Horde and the Khanates on the banks of the Volga River was provoked by the forced Islamization led by Uzbeg Khan (1312–42). Despite their exodus, this group eventually came to renounce paganism and embrace Islam. Grand Duke Vytautas of Lithuania (1392–1430) granted the Tatar settlers land and privileges, including freedom of religion, in exchange for military service, especially against the Teutonic Knights: these former crusaders in the Holy Land sought to settle on Polish and Lithuanian soil under the pretext of fighting Lithuanian pagans.

The second stage of settlement occurred between the sixteenth and eighteenth centuries: it consisted first of prisoners captured during the war with the Crimean Horde, and subsequently of civilians from the Kazan and Astrakhan Khanates who fled from Russian occupation. By the end of the seventeenth century, King John III Sobieski (1629–96) granted the Tatar settlers *demesnes* ('areas of land') in the Podlasie district.

The Qurʾāns of the GDL Tatars

The still preserved manuscripts of the Qurʾān are among the most abundant written artefacts produced by the Tatars of the Grand Duchy of Lithuania (GDL). They are surpassed in number only by prayer books (*chamails*) that contain various texts on religious themes: practical descriptions of Muslim rituals, including ablutions, prayers, rites of the life cycle (name giving, circumcision, marriage), charts with the Muslim calendar, and in some cases magical texts, which also often feature fragments of the Qurʾān. These Qurʾānic manuscripts

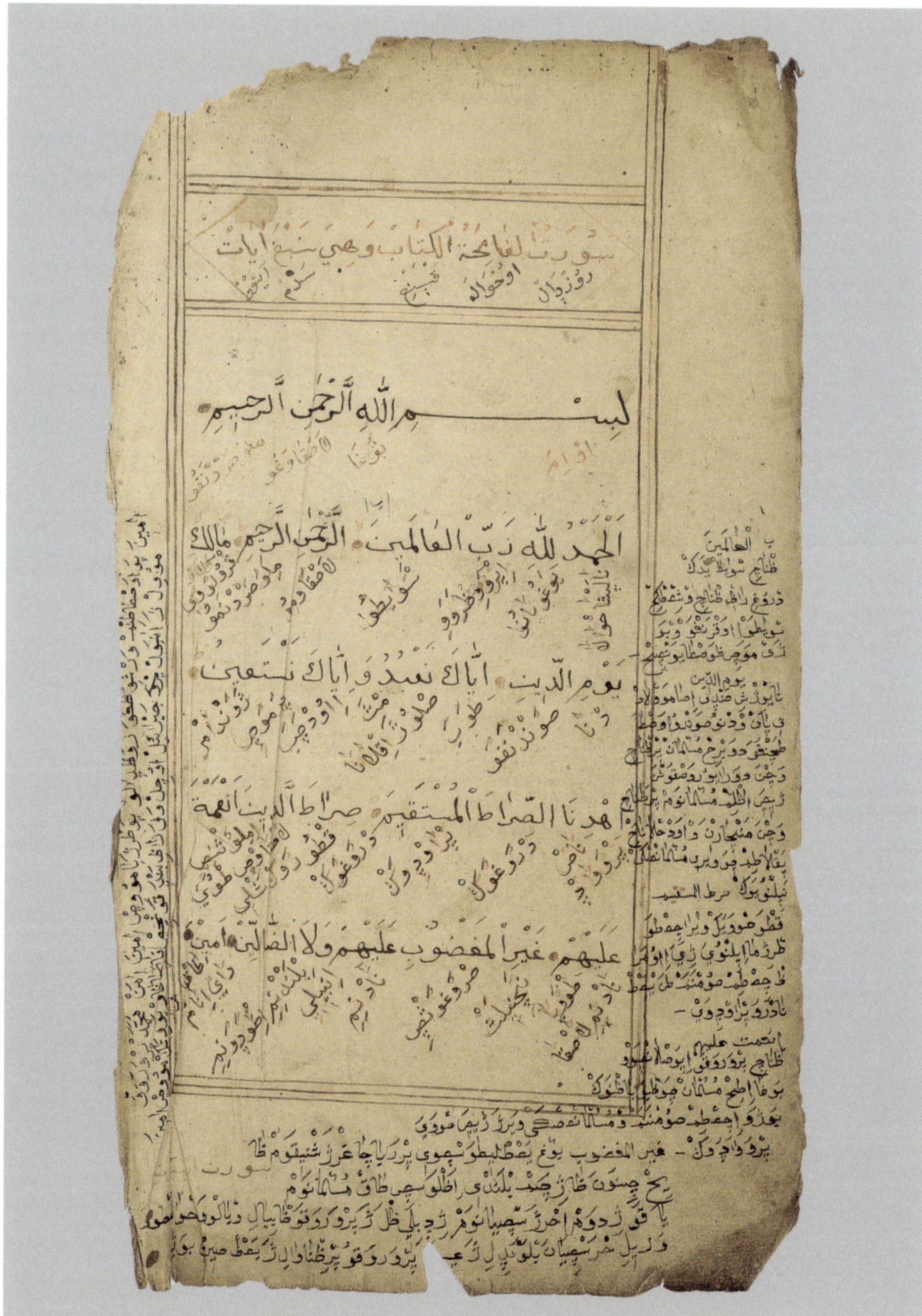
سورة الفاتحة الكتاب وهي سبع ايات

بسم الله الرحمن الرحيم

الحمد لله رب العالمين الرحمن الرحيم مالك

يوم الدين اياك نعبد واياك نستعين

اهدنا الصراط المستقيم صراط الذين انعمت

عليهم غير المغضوب عليهم ولا الضالين امين

Fig. 8: *Jabłoński's Tefsir* ('*Tefsir* of the Tatars'), 1723. Lithuania, private collection, fol. 1v

contain not only the full text of the Holy Book in Arabic but also prayers and guidelines for correct recitation. Occasionally they include lists of intentions or selected fragments, particularly the text of the 36th sura, *Ya-Sin*, which is recited at funerals. The Morisco communities described above also included *Ya-Sin* in their Qur'ānic compilations and selections. The popularity of this sura illustrates the great importance of funeral rites for those who live in minority enclaves, far from the lands of Islam. Numerous handwritten copies of the Qur'ān have survived to this day, preserved in private collections as well as the Lithuanian National Museum in Vilnius and the Belarusian National Museum of History of Religion in Grodno. These copies date from the end of the sixteenth to the early nineteenth centuries.

When the Tatars first took up residence in the Grand Duchy of Lithuania (GDL), we should keep in mind that they read Muslim literature in Turkish, brought by settlers in the fourteenth and fifteenth centuries or acquired later. Around 1620, testimony from a former Turkish captive indicates that the Tatars of the GDL had begun translating the Qur'ān into the language of the 'non-believing' Poles, although they used Arabic script, therefore a sort of 'Aljamiado'. The process of linguistic assimilation is estimated to have lasted from the sixteenth to the first half of the seventeenth century, resulting in the use of Polish and Belarusian (but not Lithuanian) as the vehicular languages of the diaspora. As an interesting rule, texts were always translated from Arabic to Polish and from Turkish to Belarusian; the Qur'ān was rendered into borderland Polish dialects – based on Polish overlapping with a Belarusian and Lithuanian substrate – which were gradually established in the territory of the GDL after 1569. As translating the Qur'ān from Arabic into any other language was a highly polemical issue, the full text of the Qur'ān with an interlinear, oblique translation into Polish was labelled as *Tefsir*, alluding to the classic Arabic tradition of *tafsīr*, Qur'ānic commentaries that elaborate on the religious meaning of the sacred text. To date, twenty-six *Tefsir* manuscripts have been identified. The earliest dates to the late sixteenth century and is a translation into Turkish (**fig. 7**).
The next *Tefsir* (1686) contains a Turkish translation of the first eighteen suras and a Polish translation of the rest of the Qur'ān. According to the colophon, the translator and copyist was Uryash ibn Ismail, Imam of Minsk, an otherwise unknown figure. All later *Tefsirs* are Polish translations or variations of the same translation. The original translation was made by an unknown translator, possibly in the late sixteenth or early seventeenth century. The translation from Arabic is heavily mediated by Turkish exegetical material (**fig. 8**).

The oldest complete copy of this translation is the *Tefsir* from Alytus, also called *Jabłoński's Tefsir*, dated 1723. It should be noted that while the original part of the translation dates to the early eighteenth century, its corrected, supplemented, and added fragments date from 1836. The exact date of the copy is provided in the colophons in Polish and Arabic. Thanks to the colophon, we know that the copyist was Izmael Jabłoński, son of Mustafa. Imam Ibrahim Januszewski later expanded, supplemented, and modernized the text. In the nineteenth century, the manuscript belonged to Samuel Ułan, a co-organizer of a Tatar squadron in the Napoleonic army in 1812. Today the manuscript is part of a private collection in Lithuania. In addition to the *Tefsir* text, it contains prayers that are recited at the beginning and end of Qurʾānic recitation, a list of intentions, and some private notes. Marginal glosses, written in the Latin alphabet, attest to the GDL Tatars' interest in Biblical literature, examined to find information that would complement Islamic sources.

The 1890 translation, called *Jozefowicz's Tefsir*, contains the same translation as the one in the manuscript mentioned before. The copyist was Adam Jozefowicz, and it was commissioned by Adam Mahamet Mejszutowicz.

As in the Morisco translations of the Qurʾān, in the manuscripts of the Tatars of the GDL the sacred character of the text is highlighted by the use of Arabic script, here adapted to convey the phonological features of Slavic languages. The Tatars of the GDL completed the process of adapting the alphabet by the second half of the sixteenth century. All Polish-Tatar texts were vocalized – special characters were added in order to convey the exact pronunciation of the words – and additional letters were introduced to render the text more legible. Some of these letters were of Turkish origin, while others were home-grown modifications. Interestingly, even though the pages were numbered with the western Arabic numerals current in Europe, eastern Arabic numerals were used in the main text. In addition, the manuscripts are bound in European style.

How to study the religious literature of European Muslims?

The Qurʾāns of the Moriscos and the GDL Tatars pose numerous challenges for researchers, such as deciphering the script, understanding idiosyncrasies of translation, and grappling with their liminal character. However, it is precisely these features that make them perfect examples of how European Muslims constructed their self-image in relation to their Christian neighbours. These artefacts attest to the permeability of Muslim and Christian intellectual communities, as evidenced by their glosses and annotations.

Thanks to Morisco studies, we can now appreciate the extent to which the written production of this group influenced the religious and cultural heritage of Europe. Similarly, studying the circulation of Tatar manuscripts among non-Muslim Europeans could greatly enhance our understanding of these phenomena. Taking a closer look at how Tatar readers annotated their religious texts with references to the Christian Bible reveals strategies fundamental for understanding interwoven European religiosities. Some centuries earlier, in Iberia, the Moriscos used not only Old Testament (and Qurʾānic) figures – such as Adam, Abraham, and Moses but also Jesus and Mary – to explore the points of convergence between Christianity and Islam, figures that were exploited also by Christian evangelizers. It might seem that the Moriscos sought to blur the boundaries between these two religions. Particularly in texts prepared for Christian readers, Morisco authors thought it beneficial to focus their patrons' attention on figures that were familiar from the Bible.

The attentive reading of these sources, with special attention not only to the main text but also to all forms of glosses and interlinear annotations, may prove to be of key importance. This approach may help us understand not only the religiosity of European Muslims but also the aspects of Islamic doctrine that European Christians exploited for intellectual or polemical reasons.

In conclusion, the study of the Qurʾāns of the Moriscos and the Tatars of the GDL not only provides insight into the religious lives and cultural interactions of European Muslims but also serves as a crucial lens to examine the broader dynamics of religious and cultural exchange in Europe. The unique adaptations found in these manuscripts reflect a vibrant interplay between Islamic and Christian traditions, showcasing the adaptability and resilience of these communities.

The Qurʾān as Turkish Booty (Türkenbeute)

Paul Babinski, University of Copenhagen

In the early modern period, Christian scholars sought to move beyond medieval polemics and understand Islam directly from Muslim sources, above all the Qurʾān. However, Arabic Qurʾān manuscripts were often difficult to find, and no printed edition of the work was available until 1694. Even as Islamic manuscripts began to be collected on a large scale in Western and Central Europe, Arabic Qurʾāns remained scarce, likely reflecting a particular reticence among Muslims to sell the Qurʾān to Christian travellers. As a result, we find European orientalists copying out the entirety of the Arabic text by hand well into the seventeenth century.

Many of the first Qurʾāns to circulate widely in Christian Europe arrived as war booty, above all from Hungary and South-East Europe, where the Ottomans struggled for territorial control with the Holy Roman Empire and other European powers.[1] These Qurʾāns, typically taken by soldiers after sieges and battles, arrived with waves of other looted material, so-called *Türkenbeute* ('Turkish booty'). An eighteenth-century German observer catalogued the items of a haul of loot that arrived from Belgrade. It contained numerous objects – exceptional and everyday – including a miniature Qurʾān:

> This Qurʾān was received alongside other Turkish rarities, such as a *tug* banner with a gilded silver top, and a red, yellow, and violet blue silk

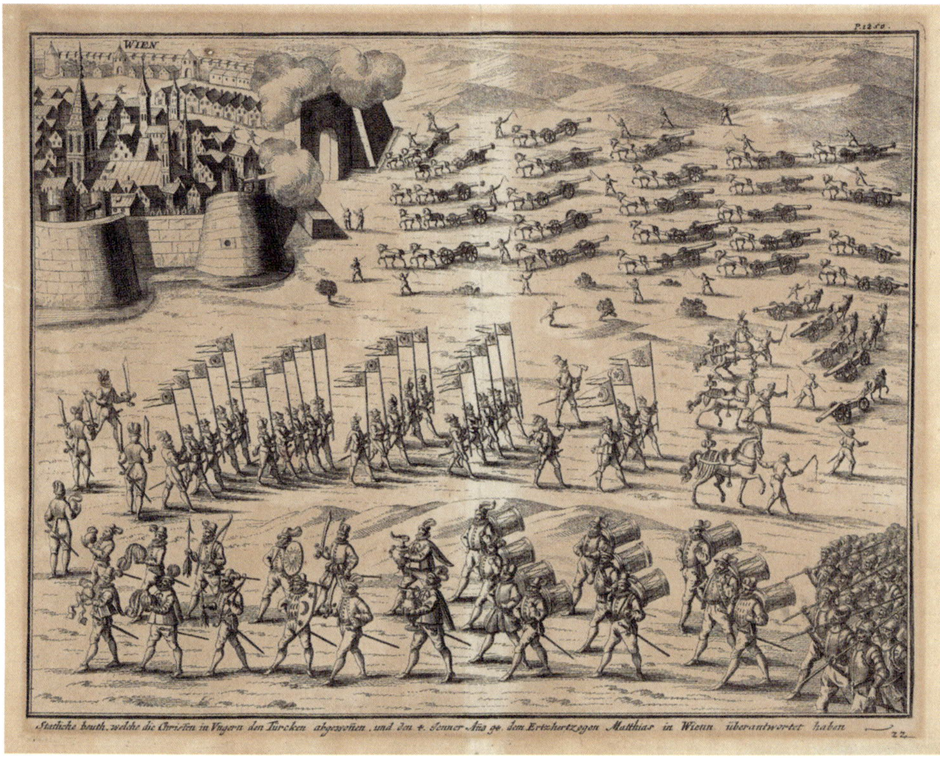

Fig. 1: Engraving from Conrad Lautenbach's trade fair report depicting the parade of *Türkenbeute* taken from the 1593 Battle of Székesfehérvár into Vienna. Wien Museum, inv. 29652

covering; the marriage contract of a pasha (among whose possessions, no doubt, the other Turkish things were found) with the daughter of a *defterdar*, three ells long, half of which is covered with partially and fully embellished circles and writing; a calendar in which is found writing, in two round discs and in between, in two columns, as well as many other books; a large book of his entries and travels; a prayer book; an exceptional seal, made of carnelian, with Arabic writing; a Turkish rosary made of amber; an inlaid knife, with gilded writing on its blade; a copper, ornamented coffee pot with gilded lid; another of Russia leather with silver stitching; a black bathing cap stitched with gold; a wooden spoon with ivory, and other household goods; a *cingulum castitatis* of human hair, from a distinguished officer after the battle and looting of Belgrade.[2]

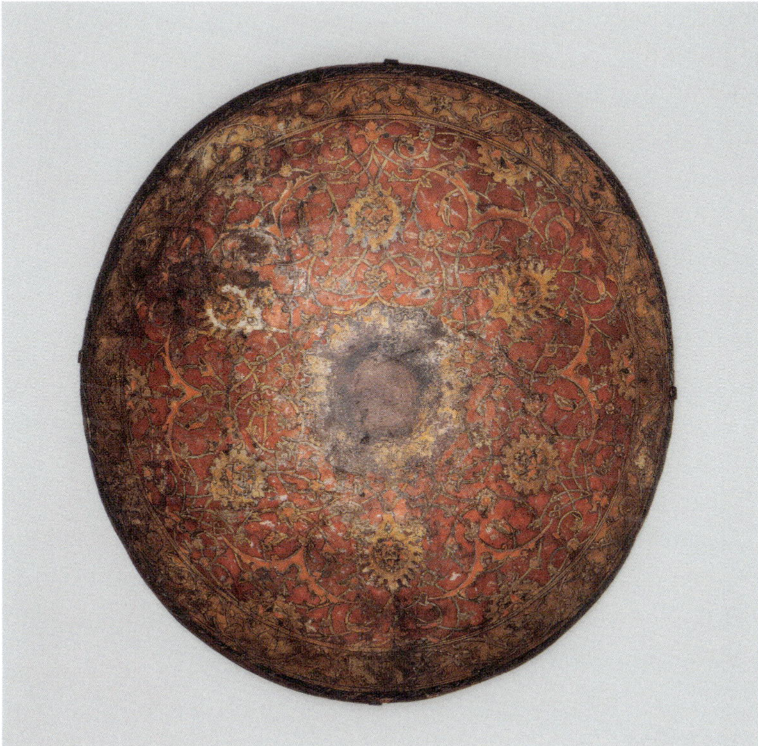

Fig. 2: Round shield with 'oriental design', Venetian, end of 16th cent. Kunsthistorisches Museum Vienna, Imperial Armoury, inv. A 2150

From the fifteenth through the eighteenth century, countless looted Qurʾāns circulated across Europe, especially in the Holy Roman Empire, where they played a particularly formative role in the study of Islam and the development of academic orientalism. Today, we typically encounter these looted objects not in their material context as war booty, but in isolation, after centuries of loss, sorting, and reclassification have deposited them into a variety of museums, libraries, and private collections.

Waves of looted *orientalia* ebbed and flowed with the changing balance of power in Europe. Through the mid-sixteenth century, Ottoman armies under Süleyman I made steady gains into Europe, taking Belgrade in 1521, Mohács in 1526, and Buda in 1541. At that point, loot flowed from west to east, most famously with the dispersal of the library of Matthias Corvinus and items like the bronze candlesticks from the Matthias Church in Buda, found today in the Hagia Sophia in Istanbul. The first major wartime dispersal of Islamic manuscripts into Europe followed Charles V's Tunis campaign in 1535, and manuscripts from Tunis soon came into the hands of European orientalists.[3] Significant amounts of looted Ottoman material, as well as Turkish captives, first arrived with the Habsburg-Ottoman Long Turkish War at the turn of the seventeenth century.

A haul of *Türkenbeute* seized early in the Long Turkish War, after a November 1593 victory at Székesfehérvár (Stuhlweißenburg), is depicted in a contemporary engraving (**fig. 1**), which illustrated a 'trade fair report' (*Meßrelation*) published by the Frankfurt theologian Conrad Lautenbach (d.1595) under the pseudonym 'Jacobus Francus'. Such reports, containing short descriptions of current events, were an important precursor of the modern newspaper, and Lautenbach's *Meßrelation* followed a successful formula, combining accounts of battles and happenings at court with stories of wonders and other curiosities. The report for 1594 offered a description of the ceremonial parade of *Türkenbeute* from Székesfehérvár into Vienna:

> At the front, the Győr quartermaster went with two Viennese assistants beside him. Then they paraded the thirty captured Turkish cannons. The largest came first: five fairly long falconets with complete carriages, on four wheels, and the other twenty-five smaller canons (*scharpffnetlein*) with inferior carriages on two wheels. Following these were three Turkish horses with saddles adorned with velvet and gilding, whose stirrups and other equipment were silver and gilded, and on which stately gilded swords were bound. 22 Turkish flags followed, of which the first three were main banners with large silver and gold threading. After that, the aforementioned two men [envoys] walked side by side, each with a gilded mace (*Pusican*) in their hand. Behind them followed many people, carrying two gilded sabres, two daggers, a helmet covered in silver and gold, an ornamented Janissary hat, a Turkish cap of golden cloth, two splendid bows, along with arrows and intricately decorated and gilded quivers, two beautiful Turkish shields, as used by the Beys and the Pashas, two long, ornamented Turkish knives, two silver and gold Turkish drinking bottles, 10 Janissary drums, and other additional things. Of these, the first two horses were designated for Emperor Rudolph II and the third for Archduke Matthias.[4]

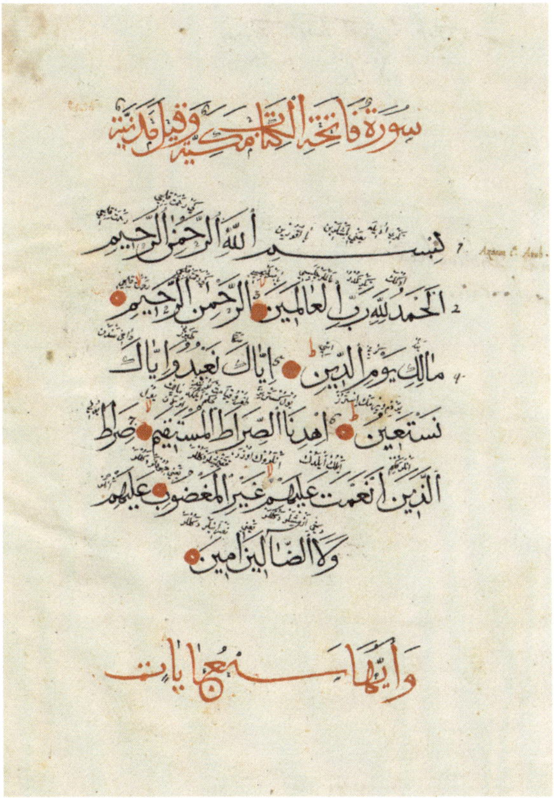
سورة فاتحة الكتاب مكية وقيل مدنية

بسم الله الرحمن الرحيم

الحمد لله رب العالمين الرحمن الرحيم

مالك يوم الدين اياك نعبد واياك

نستعين اهدنا الصراط المستقيم صراط

الذين انعمت عليهم غير المغضوب عليهم

ولا الضالين امين

وآيها سبع آيات

Fig. 3: Sebastian Tengnagel, *Qurʾān : Koran* (Istanbul, 1655). Vienna, Austrian National Library, Cod. A. F. 6, fol. 1v

The engraving is unsigned, but the artist appears to have worked from the report's description rather than eyewitness experience. This is seen in a number of small errors and discrepancies, such as the depiction of the Ottoman mace (*bozdoğan*, corrupted in German as *Pusikan*) as an axe, and the lack of distinction between forms of artillery.

The Vienna parade of *Türkenbeute* depicted in the engraving shows a growing courtly interest in orientalia as curiosities, trophies of victory, and objects of pageantry. This reflected the significance and availability of looted Ottoman objects and, at northern courts, was inspired by Italian tastes. The core of the collection of oriental weapons in the Saxon Elector's Armoury (*Rüstkammer*) in Dresden, for instance, consisted of Medici diplomatic gifts of (mostly Ottoman) weapons and armour, sent by Grand Duke Francesco I to Dresden in 1587, along with eight horses and small bronzes by Francesco's court sculptor Giambologna. Around the same time, Venetian shields imitating Islamic models were used by the bodyguard of Wolf Dietrich von Raitenau, Prince-Archbishop of Salzburg (cf. fig. 2). Such displays cemented the political significance of *orientalia* (and, more specifically, *Türkenbeute*) and helped to establish collections that expanded with later waves of lootings and efforts to purchase from abroad.

Looted manuscripts and Ottoman captives from the Long Turkish War also played a major role in the nascent tradition of academic oriental studies and the study of the Qurʾān. The librarian at Vienna's Court Library, Sebastian Tengnagel, for example, employed an Ottoman scribe, Ibrahim Derviş, who had been taken captive at Győr, and owned a number of Qurʾān sections, which appear to have been looted from the mobile library accompanying the Ottoman relief army defeated at Esztergom in 1595.[5] Tengnagel also owned a magnificent Turkish interlinear translation of the Qurʾān produced in Esztergom in 1555 (fig. 3). Another manuscript looted from Ottoman Hungary was presented in 1593 to the Heidelberg orientalist Jakob Christmann, who studied it closely. After Christmann's death, it passed to another German orientalist, Wilhelm Schickard, in Tübingen.[6]

Still, the volume of *Türkenbeute* from the Long Turkish War paled in comparison to the enormous material transfer that followed later in the century, when troops of the Holy League pressed deep into Ottoman Europe in the years following Kara Mustafa Pasha's retreat from the Siege of Vienna in 1683. Once again, loot spurred new interest in the courtly display of *orientalia*. The Saxon Elector's Armoury was a major beneficiary of looted weapons and armour, and new collections were formed in places like Karlsruhe, inspiring courts to seek out ornate Ottoman weapons and textiles.

Among these looted objects were hundreds of Islamic manuscripts, many of which offer a glimpse into both the lives of their Ottoman readers and their later circulation as *Türkenbeute*: souvenirs of victory, exotic keepsakes, and objects of study. Annotations left by Ottoman and Christian owners show that they came from a variety of sources: some were taken from individual soldiers, others from private collections,[7] and some came later with foreign merchants.[8] The largest proportion likely came from mosque and madrasa libraries, and the provenance of many can be identified on the basis of endowment notes. The Great Mosque in Buda, in particular, was a source of hundreds of *Türkenbeute* manuscripts. A large group of them was taken by Luigi Marsigli, who had assisted the siege as an

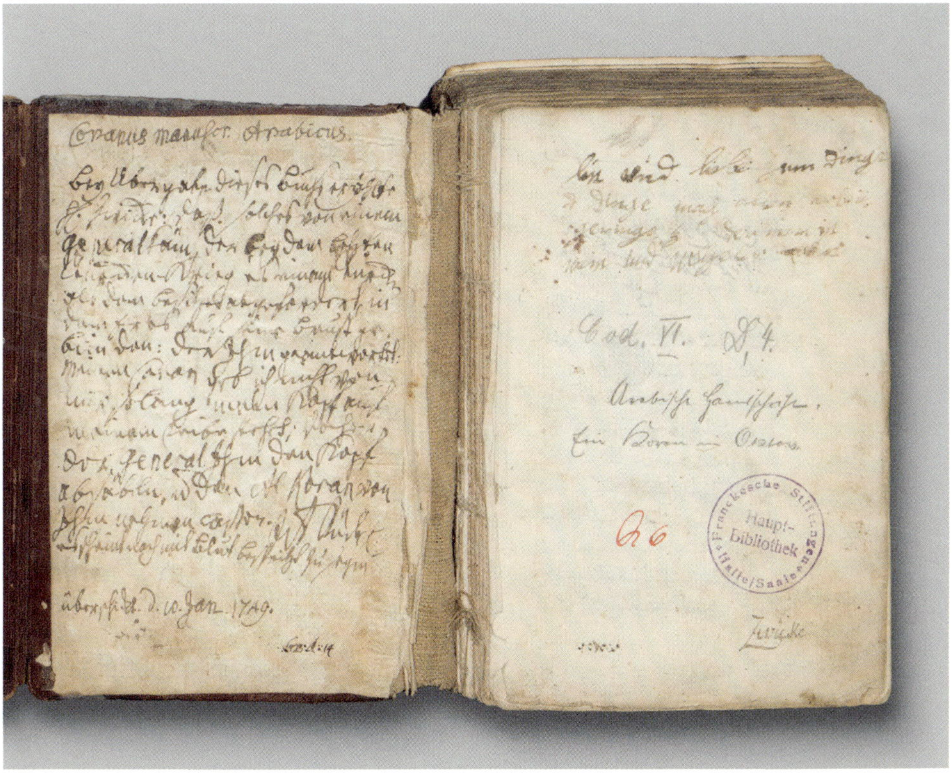

Fig. 4: Eighteenth-century flyleaf note in a Halle Qurʾān relating a story about the beheading of an Ottoman prisoner who refused to part with it. Halle, Franckesche Stiftungen, Studienzentrum August Hermann Francke, Archiv und Bibliothek AFSt/H Q 6, inside back cover

engineer, to Bologna. Others were dispersed far and wide across Europe. A looter's note in a Leipzig manuscript paints a gruesome scene of the Grand Mosque library ransacked in view of the corpse of a learned Ottoman:

> The dead body of the Turkish pontiff, whose head was pierced in the middle of the forehead by the shot of a soldier's rifle, lay prostrate on the ground in his study where I obtained this book, much like a second Archimedes, nearly buried among his countless books and manuscripts, which had been torn and strewn about by the uncultivated soldiers. It was apparent from his features that he was a man of venerable learning and a combination of courtesy and dignity.[9]

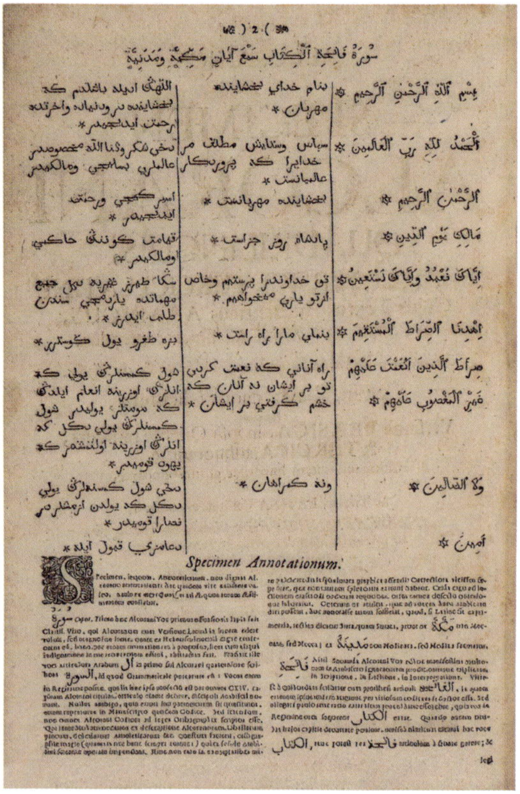

Specimen Annotationum.

Fig. 5: Acoluthus's specimen of his polyglot Qurʾān *Tetrapla Alcoranica Sive Specimen Alcorani* (Berlin, 1701). Munich, Bayerische Staatsbibliothek, 2 A.or. 38, 2

The note's staged recognition of common humanity contrasts with its almost fetishist conferral of status as a grisly relic of extraordinary violence (the massacres that followed the Siege of Buda were notoriously brutal). A *Türkenbeute* inscription in another manuscript likely looted from the same place goes even further, remarking succinctly that it was 'extracted, covered in blood, from under the corpse of the slain Mufti of Buda.'[10]

A later inscription in a *Türkenbeute* Qurʾān reveals how a certain fascination with an aura of violence around *Türkenbeute* manuscripts persisted. In 1749, Johann Abraham Rüdel, then helping to oversee the Halle Orphanage, recorded on the flyleaf of a recently donated Qurʾān a third-hand story about its history:

> Handing over this book, Mr Zwicke recounted that it came from a general who demanded it from a Turk during the last Turkish War, [as he had it] bound to his chest. The Turk answered: "I will not give up my Qurʾān as long as my head is on my body." So the General chopped off his head and had the Qurʾān taken from him. It still seems to be stained with blood.[11]

Despite the reference to an apparent blood stain, the vague details do little to bolster the story's veracity. Nonetheless, they offer a sense of the legends and oral traditions that surrounded *Türkenbeute* manuscripts (cf. fig. 4).

Looted manuscripts and the military victories that gave rise to looting spurred new interest in the Qurʾān. Perhaps no scholar benefited more from these developments than the Breslau orientalist Andreas Acoluthus, who bought up countless *Türkenbeute* manuscripts on his travels, and sometimes received them as gifts from friends and strangers. Among others, Acoluthus owned a Qurʾān with an endowment note from the Gül Baba complex in Buda, and even one that had been taken from a mosque in Sulawesi.[12] With dozens of Qurʾān manuscripts – mostly looted – at his disposal, and with the help of at least one Turkish assistant who had probably been a captive, Acoluthus began working on an unfinished Latin-Arabic-Turkish-Persian polyglot Qurʾān (fig. 5).[13] However, Acoluthus was just one of a host of German scholars who turned to studying the Qurʾān in response to the availability of looted manuscripts, including Abraham Hinckelmann, who produced the first widely available printed edition of the Arabic Qurʾān, and Matthias Friedrich Beck, who produced an annotated edition of two Qurʾānic suras.[14]

Türkenbeute made up only a small portion of the tens of thousands of Islamic manuscripts that were collected in Western and Central Europe before 1800. Most were acquired through networks of trade and diplomacy, often with the help of brokers and middlemen in centres of the Ottoman book trade, like Cairo and Istanbul. Nevertheless, looted manuscripts and captive Ottomans played a significant role in the early development of oriental studies and, especially after 1700, were instrumental in the growing European prominence of German *Orientalistik* ('Oriental Studies'), which soon flourished in places (like Halle and Leipzig) that had benefitted from looted collections. Even into the nineteenth century, orientalist Qurʾānic studies relied on *Türkenbeute*, including manuscripts used in Heinrich Leberecht Fleischer's landmark edition of al-Bayḍāwī's Qurʾān commentary and Gustav Flügel's edition of the Arabic Qurʾān.

1 On the role of looted manuscripts in the history of European Qurʾānic studies, see Paul Babinski and Jan Loop, 'Looting and Learning: War and the Qurʾān in European Oriental Studies', *Erudition and the Republic of Letters 9* (2024), forthcoming.

2 Johann Christian Kundmann, *Rariora Naturae et Artis item in Re Medica, oder Seltenheiten der Natur und Kunst des Kundmannischen Naturalien-Kabinets, wie auch in der Artzeney-Wissenschaft* (Breslau and Leipzig, 1737), 708–09: 'Diesen Alcoran habe nebst andern Türkischen Seltenheiten: Als einen Roß Schweiff mit einem vergoldeten silbernen Knopff, nebst dessen seidenen roth, gelb und violet blauen invulcro; Einen Heuraths-Contract eines Bassa (bey welchen unfehlbar auch die andern Türckischen Sachen angetroffen worden,) mit der Tochter eines Deffterdars, so 3. Ellen lang, die Helffte mit gantz und halb umschriebenen Circuln und Schrifft; it. Einen Calender, darinnen in 2. runten Scheiben und darzwischen in zweyen Columnen Schrifft sich befindet, und viele andere Scripturen; it. ein grosses Buch von seinen Intraden und Reisen; ein Gebet Buch; einige vortreffliche Siegelsteine von Carneol mit Arabischer Schrifft; einen Türckischen Rosen-Crantz von Birnstein; ein Einlege-Messer, da auf der Klinge goldene Schrifft; einen kupffern und verzienten Caffée – Krug mit vergoldeten Deckel; it. einen anderen von Juchten mit Silber gesticket; eine schwartz mit Gold gestickte Bade-Mütze; einen höltzernen Esse-Löffel unten mit Elffenbein und anderen Haußrath; it. einen cingulo castitatis von Menschen-Haaren nach emportirung Belgrads und gewonnenen Schlacht davor, von einem vornehmen Officier erhalten.'

3 See Laura Hinrichsen, 'The Circulation of Arabic Books from Ifrīqiya in Europe after the Sack of Tunis (1535)', *Erudition and the Republic of Letters* 9 (2024), forthcoming.

4 Conrad Lautenbach, *Jacobi Franci Relacio. Historica Quinquennalis Wahrhafftige beschreibung* (Frankfurt a.M., 1601), 402: 'Fornen her gieng der Zeugwart von Raab/ und neben ihm zween Wienerische Zeug Diener. Darauff hat man die dreissig eroberte Türkische stück Geschütz geführet/ allwegen die grösten voran/ als 5. zimliche lange Falckonet/ mit ihren gantzen Gefessen/ auff vier Rädern/ und die andern fünff und zwäntzig/ so scharpffnetlein mit ihren schlimmen Gefessen auff zwey Rädern. Nach denselbigen drey Türckische Roß mit sammeten beschlagenen vergülten Sätlen/ deren Stägreiff und ander Gezeug silbern und vergült gewesen/ sampt angebundenen stattlichen vergülten Pallaschen. Folgend die 22. Türckische Fahnen/ darunter die ersten drey Häuptfahnen/ mit grossen silbern und vergülten Knüpffen/ Darauff sind obbemeldte zween abgesandte Herren neben einander gangen/ deren jeder einen vergülten Pusican in der Hand geführet/ denen viel Personen nachgefolget/ so zween vergülte Säbel/ zween Stecher/ ein gantz silberne vergülte Sturmhauben/ einen beschlagenen Janitscher Hut/ ein Türckische Hauben von güldenem stück/ zween herrliche Bogen mit iren Pfeilen/ deren Köcher uberaus von schöner Arbeit beschlagen und vergült/ zwo Türckische schöne Rudelen/ wie es die Beegen und Bassen inen vor führen lassen, Item/ zwey lange Türckische beschlagene Messer/ zwo silbern und vergüldte Türckische Trinckfläschen/ 10. Janitscher Trummeln/

und andere mehr Sachen getragen/ Darvon die ersten zwei geführte Roß der Kays. May. Rudolpho 2. und das dritte Ertzhertzog Matthiae deputirt gewesen.'

5 On Tengnagel and the Esztergom manuscripts, see Claudia Petrolini, 'Captive books, captive teachers. Spoils of the Long Turkish Wars in 17th-century Vienna', *Erudition and the Republic of Letters* 9 (2024), forthcoming.

6 Oxford, Bodleian Library, ms Laud. or. 246.

7 *Türkenbeute* inscriptions mentioning private libraries are particularly rare. A notable exception is SBB-PK, ms Diez A fol. 59, a copy of an Ottoman medical work (*Yādigār-i Ibn Šerīf*) with a Latin note by a certain David Heinrich von Schmettau, remarking that he had taken it, along with other manuscripts, from the home of the Ottoman master of fortifications in Buda.

8 Andreas Acoluthus notes that he purchased B. or. 175 from Greek merchants in Vienna.

9 Leipzig University Library, ms B. or. 104, f. Iv: 'Pontificis Turcici cadaver mortuum, cujus caput in medio frontis sclopeto militari seuitia erat perforatum in museo suo ubi hoc libro sum potitus in terra prostratum jacebat et instar alterius Archimedis inter innumerum fere librorum et manuscriptorum suorum a literarum imperito milite dilaceratorum et dissipatorum catervam quasi sepultum inveniebatur. Vir, uti ex lineamentis exanimati poterat colligi, cultu venerabilis et comitate gravitate mixta conspicuus fuerat.'

10 Gotha Research Library, ms Arab. 3: 'Budae sub cadavero occisi Mufti extractum multo sanguine aspersum'.

11 Frankesche Stiftungen – Halle, ms Q 6. See Simon Mills, '*Türkenbeute* in Halle: The Spoils of War and the Study of Islam in an Eighteenth-Century Pietist Orphanage', *Erudition and the Republic of Letters 9* (2024), forthcoming: 'Bey Ubergabe dieses Buchs erzählte H[err] Zwicke: daß solches von einem General käm, der bey dem letzten Türcken-Krieg es einem Türcken als dem Besitzer abgefordert, in dem Er es auf seine Brust gebunden: Der Ihm geantwortet: Meinen Coran geb ich nicht von mir solang mein Kopf auf meinem Leibe stehet; Daher der General Ihm den Kopf absäbeln. u[nd] den Al Koran von Ihm nehmen laßen. es scheint noch mit Blut bespritzt zu seyn überschickt. d. 10. Jan. 1749. J. A. Rüdel'.

12 Leipzig University Library, mss B. or. 162, 130.

13 This helper is mentioned in Copenhagen Kongelige Bibliotek, Bøll. Brevsamling, U 4°, n. 376. Groddeck to Picques: 'Mr. Acoluth à Breslau travaille à présent à une nouvelle edition de l'Alcoran, qu'il publiera en Arabe, Perse, Turc et Latin, par quelle raison il alimente dans sa maison un homme Turc assez sçavant selon la coutume de son pais.' ('Mr Acoluth in Breslau is working at present on a new edition of the Alcoran, which he will publish in Arabic, Persian, Turkish, and Latin, on account of which he keeps in his house a Turkish man who is fairly learned according to the customs of his land.').

14 See Asaph Ben-Tov, 'The Great Turkish War and the Study of the Qurʾān the case of Matthias Friedrich Beck (1649–1701)', *Erudition and the Republic of Letters* 9 (2024), forthcoming.

The Qurʾān and Christian Polemics in the Sixteenth and Seventeenth Century

Asaph Ben-Tov, University of Hamburg

One way of thinking about pre-modern Christian-Muslim polemics is to imagine a furious inter-religious tennis match. Apart from its adversarial nature, this metaphor, with its back and forth, also illustrates the dialectics of such interactions. In an age when religious convictions were usually claimed as certainties and divergence as error, such metaphorical tennis matches were almost inevitable. At the same time, our tennis players, engaged in a reciprocal activity, have much in common and agree, at least vaguely, on the rules of the game. If our players are any good, each will be an attentive observer of his opponent and each strike a reaction to the latter's last move. Leaving aside the question of who plays the umpire in these matches, we should note that inter-religious polemics could be heated and mean-spirited, yet often constituted a genuine dialogue. This metaphor, however, obscures a central aspect of Christian polemical readings of the Qurʾān in the sixteenth and seventeenth centuries: it presumes a coherent and unified Christianity waging a polemical war against a coherent and unified Islam. This was never the case. At least from a pre-modern Christian perspective, our 'tennis player' was going through a series of existential crises of profound consequence for why and how the match was played.

The sixteenth and seventeenth centuries witnessed an unprecedented interest in the Qur'ān in Christian Europe. This coincided with the fracturing of Latin Christendom in the Reformation and the emergence of competing – and occasionally warring – Christian denominations: the Catholic Church and several Protestant Churches with rival claims to being the one True Church. This confessional divide in Central and Western Europe was not restricted to theology but had far-reaching social and political consequences. The period also witnessed further challenges to orthodox Christianity (of all denominations), arising from new forms or radical thought, such as Socinianism which denies the Trinity or Deism which advocates a rational natural religion. These developments also influenced Christian readings of the Qur'ān and the polemics they engendered.

Furthermore, the period between the late fifteenth and the close of the seventeenth century also witnessed dramatic shifts in the political and military fortunes of Muslim and Christian powers. This timeframe begins in 1492 with the Catholic conquest of Granada, the last Muslim stronghold in the Iberian Peninsula, with tragic consequences for Spain's Muslim and Jewish communities. At the same time in the East, the Ottoman Empire, having extinguished the Byzantine Empire in 1453, was making inroads into the Balkans and further into Europe. Suffice it here to mention the Ottoman victory in the Battle of Mohács (1526), which left Suleiman the Magnificent as the ruler of much of Hungary, followed by the conquest of Buda in 1541. The Ottomans famously laid siege to Vienna in 1529. Although their attempt to conquer the Habsburg city was staved off, it sent shock waves throughout Europe. For much of the sixteenth century, the Ottomans seemed invincible. The period ended with an historic shift, beginning with a second Ottoman Siege of Vienna in the autumn of 1683. In a dramatic reversal of fortune, the Habsburgs and their allies defeated the Ottomans outside the gates of the city and went on the offensive. The ensuing Great Turkish War ended in 1699 with Hungary and further portions of the European Ottoman territories ceded to European powers. The Ottomans were still a power to be reckoned with, yet the fear of the 'Turkish menace', which in the sixteenth century was often seen in apocalyptic terms, was rapidly becoming a thing of the past.[1] Revealingly, Christians often referred to the Qur'ān as the 'Turkish Bible', with 'Turk' commonly used as a synonym for Muslim throughout this period. Polemicizing against the Qur'ān was not a detached scholarly pastime, but also a reaction to a very real and daunting Ottoman adversary.

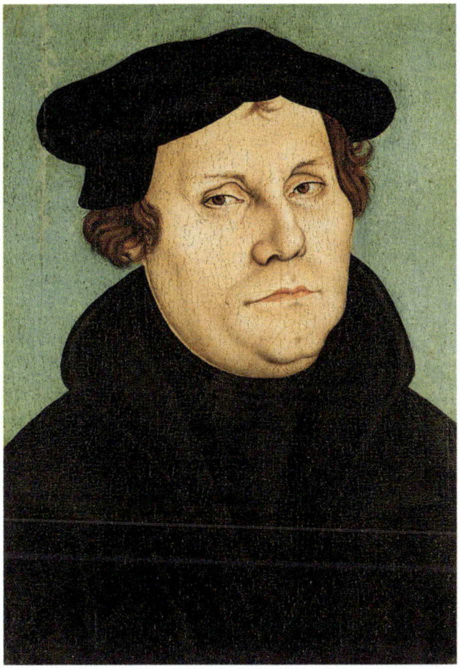

Fig. 1: Lucas Cranach the Elder, *Martin Luther*, 1528

The Qurʾān itself was only gradually made accessible to European readers. Arabic Qurʾān manuscripts were not readily available in the early sixteenth century – and very few would have been able to read them. The first ever printed edition of the entire Qurʾān in Arabic which was available to a broad readership was not published until 1694. As late as in 1530, the Protestant Reformer Martin Luther (1483–1546) complained about not being able to obtain a Qurʾān translation (**fig. 1**).[2] In 1542, Luther translated *Contra legem Sarracenorum* ('Against the Law of the Saracens') by the Franciscan Friar Ricoldo da Monte di Croce (1243–1320),[3] a polemical work on the Qurʾān still popular in the sixteenth century. In the introduction Luther writes:

> I would gladly have read the Qurʾān itself and was amazed that it had not already been translated into Latin long ago. Muhammad has held sway now for more than nine hundred years and has caused great harm, and yet no one has yet applied himself to finding out what Muhammad's faith was.

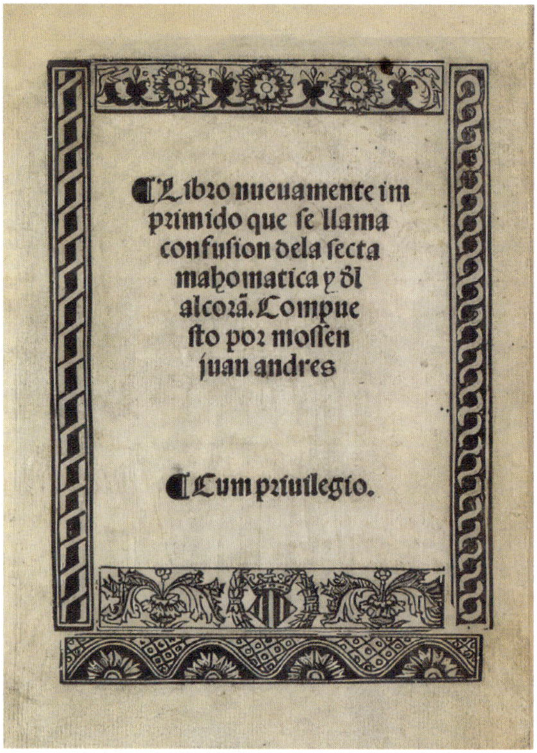

Fig. 2: Title page of Juan Andrés, *Confusión o confutación de la secta Mahomética y del Alcorán*, 1515

> ... How [else] will one be able to convert [Muslims], who reject both the Old and New Testaments ... and seal their ears, eyes and hearts against the blessed Holy Scripture and remain loyal to the Alcoran ...

Needless to say, Luther was wrong. The Qurʾān had been translated into Latin (more than once) – most important was the translation by Robert of Ketton (1143), which the Reformer would soon get to know.[4] Luther's mistake indicates the limited availability of manuscripts of Qurʾān translations. It is also revealing that anti-Qurʾānic writings like Ricoldo's or the more recent *Cribratio Alkorani* ('The Sifting of the Qurʾān') by Nicholas of Cusa (1401–64),[5] which Luther knew, were, for a long time, by far more readily available in Europe than the Qurʾān itself. A further polemical work which remained popular well into the seventeenth century was the *Confusión o confutación de la secta Mahomética y del Alcorán* ('Confusion or Confutation of the Mohammedan Sect and of the Qurʾān'; **fig. 2**), which emerged within a distinctly Iberian context.[6] Its author, Juan Andrés (c. 1450–after 1515), originally Ibn ʿAbdallah, was born near Valencia and was a Muslim *faqīh* (jurist) until his conversion to Christianity in 1487. After his baptism, he became an active missionary among his former co-religionists. In 1515, he published his *Confusión*, which went through several Spanish editions and also appeared in Latin, French, Italian, German, Dutch, and English. Much of this work repeats classic Christian arguments. At the same time, Juan Andrés makes use of his knowledge of the Qurʾān, Muslim history, and jurisprudence to convince Muslims of the errors in their ways:

> From whence thou mayest know *O Moore*, that the *Alcoran* is not the word of God, because that the word of God is as God himself, and none can nullifye God or his word. ... And how can it be authentick, seeing *Muhamed* during all the time of the twenty three years (in which he was giving the Law and making the *Alcoran*) alwayes altered the verses, and commanded them to doe many things by authority of the verses of the *Alcoran* and afterwards commanded the clean contrary, and to that purpose gave authority by other verses which revoked the former verses ... and thus I say that for these reasons *Muhamed* never commanded that his *Alcoran* should be collected or reduced into bookes and Chapters, as now it is, but kept it in the said scrowles or papers in the aforesaid ark or shrine, and many of them were lost and could never be found.[7]

Interested in Islam (and its refutation), Luther insisted that it was essential to become familiar with the Qurʾān in order to successfully convert the 'Turks'. It was a conviction he shared, amongst others, with the twelfth-century abbot of Cluny, Peter the Venerable (c.1092–1156), who commissioned a Latin translation of the Qurʾān from the above-mentioned Robert of Ketton. Four hundred years later, and shortly after Luther complained of the lack of Latin translations of the Qurʾān, Ketton's work would appear in print in Basel (1543). In fact, it was to a great extent thanks to Luther's intervention that the city council allowed for this Latin Qurʾān (the first ever printed edition of the Qurʾān in any language) to appear. Both Luther and his Wittenberg colleague, Philipp Melanchthon, wrote a preface, endorsing this edition prepared by the learned Zurich theologian Theodor Bibliander (1509–64). Both made clear that their championing

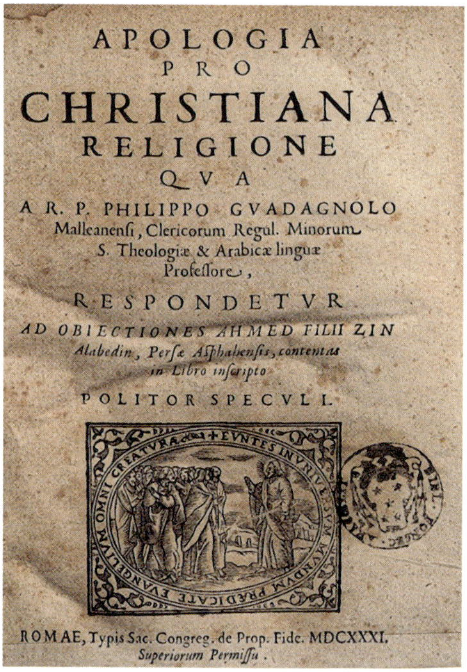

APOLOGIA
PRO
CHRISTIANA
RELIGIONE
QVA
A R. P. PHILIPPO GVADAGNOLO
Malleanensi, Clericorum Regul. Minorum
S. Theologiæ & Arabicæ linguæ
Professore,
RESPONDETVR
*AD OBIECTIONES AHMED FILII ZIN
Alabedin, Persæ Asphahensis, contentas
in Libro inscripto*
POLITOR SPECVLI.

ROMAE, Typis Sac. Congreg. de Prop. Fide. MDCXXXI.
Superiorum Permissu.

Fig. 3: Title page of Filippo Guadagnoli, *Apologia pro Christiana religione*, 1631

of the publication of the Qurʾān for Christian readers did not signify their approval of it. In fact, Luther and other Protestants occasionally referred to the 'two Antichrists': Muhammad in the East and the Pope in the West. Reading the Qurʾān was to know one's enemy.

The Basel Qurʾān was followed in the sixteenth and seventeenth centuries by a series of Latin and vernacular translations, many of them prefaced by strong-worded condemnations of the book. In some cases, this may have been lip service meant to counter accusations of publishing a blasphemous book. For all its ambivalence concerning Judaism and Christianity, the Qurʾān contains several teachings and polemical passages, which for early modern Christians were blasphemous. In other cases, the accompanying polemics were clearly meant in earnest. A good example of the latter is offered by the first English Qurʾān which appeared in London in 1649. The translation itself was made from the recent French version by André Du Ryer (1647). The English Qurʾān was prefaced, among other things, by *A needful Caveat or Admonition for them who desire to know what use may be made of, or if there be danger in reading the Alcoran* by Alexander Ross (c.1590–1654), who bleakly introduces Muslim Scripture to English readers:

> Good Reader, the great *Arabian* Impostor now at last after a thousand years, is by the way of *France* arrived in *England*, and his *Alcoran*, or gallimaufry of Errors … hath learned to speak *English*.

After this opening salvo, Ross's invectives intensify. The Qurʾān is likened by him to a monster. Just as the sight of some freak of nature, he argues, makes observers grateful to God for not creating them in such fashion, so reading the Qurʾān will make Christians all the more grateful to God for their true religion. While the underlying argument is a defence of this English publication of the Qurʾān, Ross makes his contempt for the book abundantly clear. Toward the end of the *Admonition*, he writes:

> The reading of the *Alcoran* will enable us to beat *Mahomet* with his own weapons, to cut off the head of this *Goliath* with his own Sword, and to wound this unclean bird with quills pickt out of his own wings, for even unwittingly and unwillingly he is forced to acknowledge many truths of Christian Religion, in affirming there is but one true God the Creator of all things, and though he goeth about to overthrow the Doctrine of the Trinity, yet he doth plainly confirm it … though he laboureth to overthrow the Gospel, yet he confirms it … In reading the Alcoran, though we find much dung, yet in it we shall meet with some gold …

Ross is traversing a well-trodden path. Beside supposed absurdities, the Qurʾān contains several truths, such as claims which appeared to Ross and others to echo Christian teachings.

The idea that the Qurʾān contains some Christian truth, despite its open rejection of central Christian tenets, was taken by numerous writers, both Catholic and Protestant, not so much as a bridge for inter-faith understanding but as an Achilles heel. One example for this is offered by the Jesuit Michel Nau in his *Religio Christiana contra Alcornaum per Alcoranum pacifice defensa et probata* (1680, 'Christianity Peacefully Defended and Vindicated Against the Qurʾān and through the Qurʾān'). Had he lived long enough to see it, the Scottish Protestant

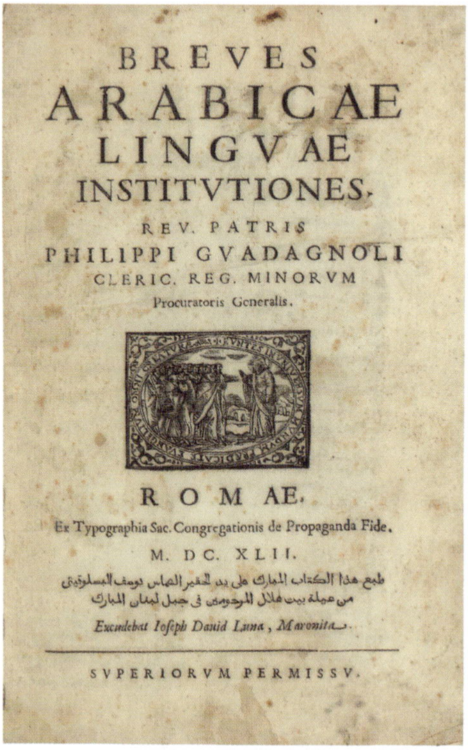
BREVES
ARABICAE
LINGVAE
INSTITVTIONES,
REV. PATRIS
PHILIPPI GVADAGNOLI
CLERIC. REG. MINORVM
Procuratoris Generalis.

ROMAE.
Ex Typographia Sac. Congregationis de Propaganda Fide.
M. DC. XLII.
طبع هذا الكتاب المبارك على يد الحقير الشماس يوسف البسلوقيني
من عيلة بيت هلال المرحومين في جبل لبنان المبارك
Excudebat Ioseph David Luna, Maronita.

SVPERIORVM PERMISSV.

Fig. 4: Title page of the Arabic version of Filippo Guadagnoli, *Apologia pro Christiana religione*, 1637

Ross would have approved of the title and of much content of the Jesuit's vindication of Christianity against the Qurʾān.

An earlier work of interfaith vindication is the *Apologia pro christiana religione* (1631, 'A Defence of Christianity') by the orientalist and Cleric Regular Minor, Filippo Guadagnoli (1596–1656; **fig. 3**). Guadagnioli contributed his knowledge of Arabic in several undertakings of the Catholic Church, including this work on a translation of the Bible into Arabic. Of all the works mentioned here, his is arguably the one that best fits the tennis metaphor. Guadagnoli's work was a direct response to the refutation of Christianity by the Persian scholar Aḥmad ibn Zayn al-ʿAbidīn (d. c.1650), which in turn was a response to a work in Persian by Jerome Xavier (1549–1617), a Jesuit missionary at the Mughal court. Guadagnoli's *Apologia* appeared in Arabic in 1637 (**fig. 4**). The second section of the work is entitled *De Alchorano, eiusque Auctore Mohamede* ('On the Qurʾān and its Author Muhammad'). The Catholic scholar argues – or, as he sees it, proves – that the Qurʾān cannot possibly be the Word of God, in contrast to the Christian Canon. Guadagnoli's line of argument was unlikely to convince many Muslims, even when presented in Arabic. For modern readers, this sort of polemical refutation is arguably one of the least appealing aspects of pre-modern inter-religious exchanges, and yet it is important to note that this *Apologia* is a work of considerable scholarship and the result of a careful reading of the Qurʾān in Arabic – an attentive reading by a pious seventeenth-century Italian Arabist, eager to defend the True Faith, meaning the tenets of the Roman Catholic Church.

By the end of the period covered here, in 1698, a milestone in Christian Europe's study of Islam was published: an Arabic edition of the Qurʾān with a Latin translation, and each sura accompanied by a selection of Muslim exegesis (*tafsīr*). This was the work of Ludovico Marracci (1612–1700), a Catholic priest and professor of Arabic in Rome (**fig. 5**). Much has been said about Marracci's Latin translation and his extensive use of Muslim scholarship. What interests us here is the prominent place allotted to polemics in this mammoth work of erudition. Each Qurʾānic sura is followed by a pious Christian refutation. The work itself is prefaced by a polemical (and massively learned) refutation of the Qurʾān.

Both Guadagnoli and especially Marracci's work were consulted by European scholars on both sides of the confessional divide. It is important to note, however, that the Catholic faith of these two scholars was under attack. Their main adversaries were not Muslim theologians in the Ottoman, Safavid, and Mughal Empires but Christian 'heretics' in Europe, namely Protestants. The Qurʾān was occasionally used by both Catholic and Protestants polemicists against their confessional adversaries within Christianity. A common accusation levelled against confessional adversaries was their supposed affinity to the 'Turks'. As such, Calvinists often found themselves accused of 'Turco-Calvinism', both for their anti-Catholic political alliances and their strict 'Mohammedan' iconoclasm, while Protestant polemics accused the Church of Rome of 'Turco-Papism'.[8] On other occasions, various sections of the Qurʾān were exploited for confessional polemics, with the 'Turkish Bible' serving either as a storehouse of anti-Christian 'blasphemies' (e.g., Antitrinitarian doctrines associated with Socinians) or as a (counter-intuitive) repository of Christian truths, acknowledged 'even by the Turks' but rejected by confessional adversaries. A good example for the latter is the Qurʾānic depiction of the Virgin Mary. Both Protestants and Catholics quoted Sura 19 (*Maryam*, 'Mary'). A short excerpt here will suffice:

> And you shall recount in the Book the story of Mary: how she left her people and betook herself to a solitary place to the east. [17] We sent her Our spirit in the semblance of a full-grown man. [18] And when she saw him she said: 'May the Merciful defend me from you! If you fear the Lord, [leave me and go away.'] [19] 'I am but your Lord's emissary,' he replied, 'and have come to give you a holy son.' [20] 'How shall I bear a child,' she answered, 'when I have neither been touched by any man nor ever been unchaste?' [21] 'Thus did your Lord speak,' he replied. 'That is easy enough for Me. He shall be a sign to mankind and a blessing from Ourself. This is Our decree.' [22] Thereupon she conceived him, and retired to a far-off place.

and shortly after Jesus's birth:

> [27] Carrying the child, she came to her people, who said to her: 'Mary, this is indeed a strange thing! [28] Sister of Aaron, your father was never a whoremonger, nor was your mother a harlot.' [29] She made a sign to them, pointing to the child. But they replied: 'How can we speak with a babe in the cradle?' [30] whereupon he spoke and said: 'I am the servant of God. He has given me the Book and ordained me a prophet. [31] His blessing is upon me wherever I go, and He has exhorted me to be steadfast in prayer and to give alms as long as I shall live. [32] He has exhorted me to honour my mother and has purged me of vanity and wickedness. [33] Blessed was I on the day I was born, and blessed I shall be on the day of my death and on the day I shall be raised to life. [34] Such was Jesus son of Mary. That is the whole truth, which they still doubt. God forbid that He Himself should beget a son![9]

To this we should add the ḥadīth by Abū Hurayra concerning her and Jesus's faultless birth:

> There is none born among the off-spring of Adam, but Satan touches it. A child therefore, cries loudly at the time of birth because of the touch of Satan, except Mary and her child.[10]

A claim strikingly close to the Catholic teaching of the Immaculate Conception widely quoted, not only by orientalists but by Catholic theologians (consulting the Qurʾān in Latin) and by a series of more humble Catholic preachers well

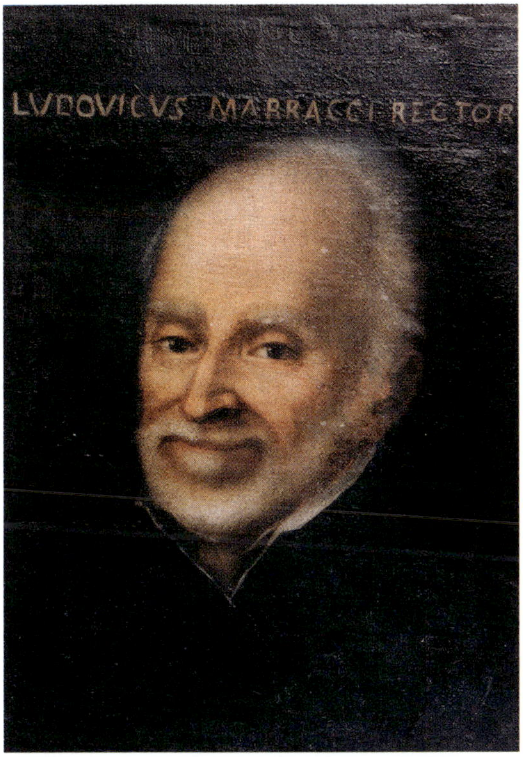

Fig. 5: Portrait of Ludovico Marracci (1612–1700)

into the eighteenth century. So did, for example, the famous Jesuit theologian Petrus Canisius (1521–97) in his *De Maria Virgine incomparabili, et Dei genitrice sacrosancta* (1577) ('On Mary the Incomparable Virgin and Most Sacred Mother of God'):

> The Mohammedans, far removed from our Christian faith as they are, are on this point superior to the Sectarians [Protestants], since they do justice to Mary and come closer to the truth and their judgment is correct. Their religion is derived from the Qurʾān and it is there that they read, are convinced thereof and wish all to be of the opinion that Mary … committed no evil her entire life, was spent her entire life in righteousness. And the following they also teach: none of the children of Adam has come into this world without being touched by Satan, except for Mary and her Son.

They steadfastly defend also this teaching: many were the perfect men, but no woman other than Mary, the Mother of Jesus.

For good measure, Canisius adds that there is no reason to feel overly grateful to Muhammad: good Christians already knew of their obligation to venerate the Holy Virgin without the Qurʾān – and yet this passage in the Qurʾān and ḥadīth was a welcome external confirmation of Chirstian (i.e., Catholic) Mariology and refutation of heretic Protestants. 'Even the Turks know better than Protestants on this matter'.

This paragraph in Canisius's massive work on the Virgin Mary was to resonate with Catholic theologians and preachers well into the eighteenth century. As late as in 1756, the German Dominican Friar Viktor Mayr fulminated from the pulpit:

> Is it possible? Would it have occurred to the mind of any reasonable man that one day anyone would dare refuse the Virgin Mary , from whom Jesus was born, here due reverence? The godless Muhammad, a sworn enemy of God and of all faith, spoke most laudably about Maria in his Qurʾān.[11]

Muhammad, for whom the Dominican had little sympathy, speaks the divine truth (on this point), while the Protestants shamelessly deny the Holy Virgin the status and reverence which 'even the Mohammedans' openly concede to her. This sort of polemics could go in either direction. Among the Qurʾānic verses less congenial to Christian readers was 5:116

> Then God will say: 'Jesus son of Mary, did you ever say to the people: "Worship me and my mother as gods besides God?"' 'Glory be to you,' he will answer, 'I could never have claimed what I have no right to.'[12]

This verse seems to suggest Mary as part of the Christian Trinity: Father, Son, and Mother. Where, some Protestant scholars asked, could Muhammad have reached such an outrageous conclusion? The answer for some was an excessive worship of Mary in late antique Arabia – still carried out in their own day by 'superstitious Catholics'. Muhammad, in other words, was reflecting the degeneration of respect for the Virgin Mary into an idolatrous worship of her – in the seventh century as in the seventeenth.

Alongside a powerful and often menacing Muslim Ottoman Empire and bitter divisions among Europe's main confessional churches, the sixteenth and seven-

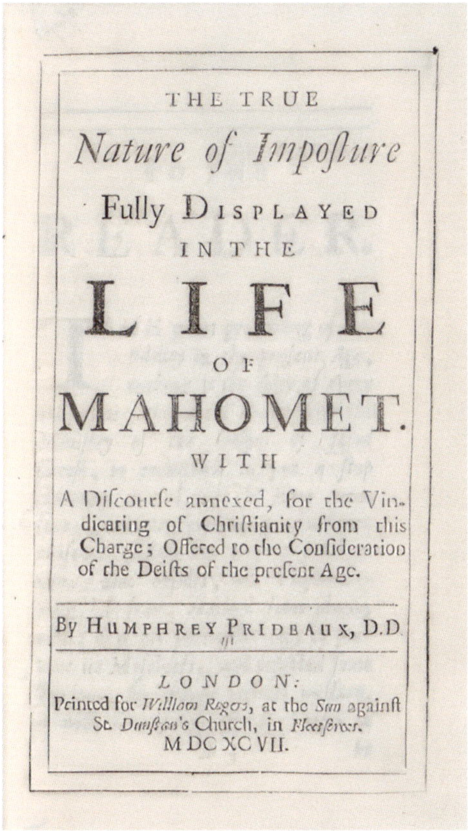

THE TRUE
Nature of Impoſture
Fully DISPLAYED
IN THE
LIFE
OF
MAHOMET.
WITH
A Diſcourſe annexed, for the Vindicating of Chriſtianity from this Charge; Offered to the Conſideration of the Deiſts of the preſent Age.

By HUMPHREY PRIDEAUX, D.D.

LONDON:
Printed for *William Rogers*, at the *Sun* againſt St. *Dunſtan's* Church, in *Fleetſtreet*.
MDCXCVII.

Fig. 6: Title page of Humphrey Prideaux, *The True Nature of Imposture*, 1697

teenth centuries also witnessed new challenges to Christian doctrine: Christian teachings clearly departing from some basic tenets of Christian orthodoxy as well as the rise of openly non-Christian religious and philosophical convictions. Perhaps the most important example of the former was Socinianism, an early modern form of Christianity which rejected the Trinity. Not surprisingly, some Socinian thinkers evinced interest in the Qurʾān. Their orthodox detractors were eager to point out the parallels between this heterodox Christian group and anti-Trinitarian teachings in the 'Turkish Bible'.[13]

Let us conclude with a case of Christian orthodox polemics, using the Qurʾān against adversaries within Europe. In 1697, Humphrey Prideaux (1648–1724),

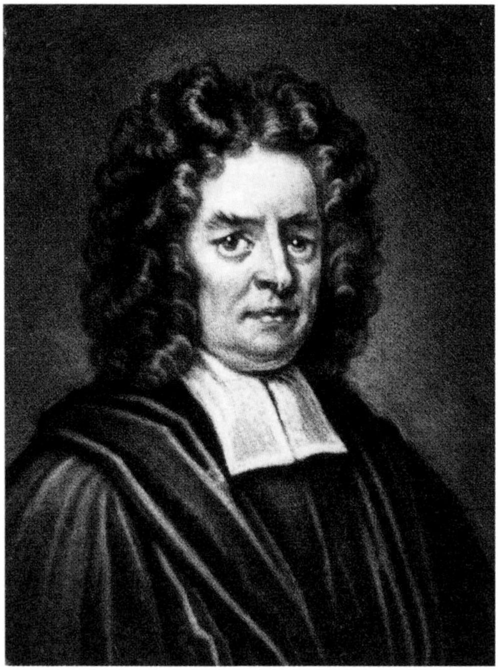

Fig. 7: Portrait of Humphrey Prideaux (1648–1724)

an Anglican churchman and scholar published his *The True Nature of Imposture fully display'd in the Life of Mahomet*, a highly polemical portrayal of the Prophet of Islam as the quintessential impostor (**figs. 6, 7**). It draws on Prideaux's not inconsiderable acquaintance with Arabic sources, including the Qurʾān itself. He was offering readers a learned, hostile and at the same time highly readable portrait of Muhammad. Not surprisingly it became a bestseller. The English edition went through numerous editions, while a French (1698 and 1699) and German (1699) translation made it available to a broader European readership. At first glance, this is yet another hostile portrayal of Muhammad and Islam – which indeed it is. And yet Prideaux's polemical intentions are more subtle. The true target of this unflattering portrayal of Muhmmad is not primarily Islam. In the English version, the biography stands between a programmatic preface and epilogue, which make the author's intention clear. As a conservative Christian clergyman in late seventeenth-century England, he was not concerned about Islam but Deism. Among certain sophisticated, non-orthodox circles, the founders of the three monotheistic religions – Moses, Jesus, and Muhammad – were all accused of being power-grabbing impostors, and Judaism, Christianity, and Islam were seen as corruptions of rational monotheism. Prideaux accepts as a matter of course that Muhammad was not a genuine prophet and that the Qurʾān was, therefore, a work of imposture. In other words, the Qurʾān was Muhammad's own invention and not the Word of God – there is nothing new or unusual in a Christian making this argument. The remarkable point is the argumentative twist the work offers. In Prideaux's line of argument, Muhammad is a quintessential case of imposture, fulfilling all the criteria which Moses and Jesus, to his mind, do not. In other words, his caustic portrayal of Muhammad, which heavily relies on his careful (if hostile) reading of the Qurʾān, is meant to vindicate Jesus and the veracity of Christianity from the attacks of sophisticated, philosophically inclined deists who saw Moses, Jesus, and Muhammad as impostors.

Both Muhammad and his early followers in seventh-century Arabia – themselves no strangers to polemics – would have been baffled by some of the polemical roles the Qurʾān had assumed in faraway Europe in the two centuries between the Reformation and the Enlightenment.

1 See Andrew Wheatcroft, *The Enemy at the Gate: Habsburgs, Ottomans and the Battle for Europe* (New York, 2008).
2 Luther makes this complaint in the introduction to his edition of George of Hungary, *De ritu et moribus turcorum* (Wittenberg, 1530, first published in Rome in 1481). On Luther and Islam, see Adam S. Francisco, *Luther and Islam* (Leiden, 2007).
3 See introduction and John Tolan's essay in this volume.
4 See Thomas E. Burman, *Reading the Qurʾān in Latin Christendom, 1140–1560* (Philadelphia, 2007).
5 See John Tolan's entry on this work.
6 On the Iberian context more generally, see Mercedes García-Arenal and Fernando Rodríguez Mediano, *The Orient in Spain*, translated by Consuelo López-Morillas (Leiden, 2013).
7 Quoted (in abridged form) from the English translation: *The Confusion of Muhamed's Sect, or a Confutation of the Turkish Alcoran; Being a Discovery of Many Secret Policies and Practices in that Religion, not Till Now Revealed*, translated by Joshua Notstock (London, 1652), 47–9.
8 See Noel Malcom, *Useful Enemies: Islam and the Ottoman Empire in Western Political Thought, 1450–1750* (Oxford, 2019).
9 Q 19:16-34, translated by N. J. Dawood.
10 Taken from the *Ṣaḥīḥ al Bukhārī*, translated by Muhammad Muhsin Khan.
11 Mayr, *Concionator panegyrico-moralis*, vol. 2 (Regensburg, 1756), 268.
12 Translated by N.J. Dawood.
13 Martin Mulsow, 'Socinianism, Islam and the Radical use of Arabic Scholarship', *Al-Qantara* 31 (2010), 549–86.

Printing the Qur'ān

Roberto Tottoli, University of Naples L'Orientale

The introduction of printing had a huge impact on the production and circulation of the Qur'ān. Although large-scale printing was only launched in the Islamic world in the second half of the nineteenth century, it caused significant changes in the production and dissemination of written copies of the Qur'ān. In line with the cultural history of many European and other civilizations, printing resulted in an unprecedented increase of written culture, further facilitated by continuous technological improvements in book production and the support of other media that allowed for the gradual expansion of the Qur'ān.

The history of printing the Qur'ān on moveable-type systems, however, did not start in the Islamic world but in Europe. Various attempts had already been made to produce the first texts in Arabic since the early sixteenth century. Printing with Arabic types was a considerable technical challenge in the early book production industry. The first Qur'ān print was made in Europe against this historical and technological backdrop. The reasons behind the actual undertaking were very complex and different from why Muslims would begin to print the Qur'ān in the nineteenth century.

Printing the Qur'ān in Europe

The cultural and linguistic interest of European intellectuals was a major factor in the growing popularity of Arabic and Islamic literary texts and, after the late

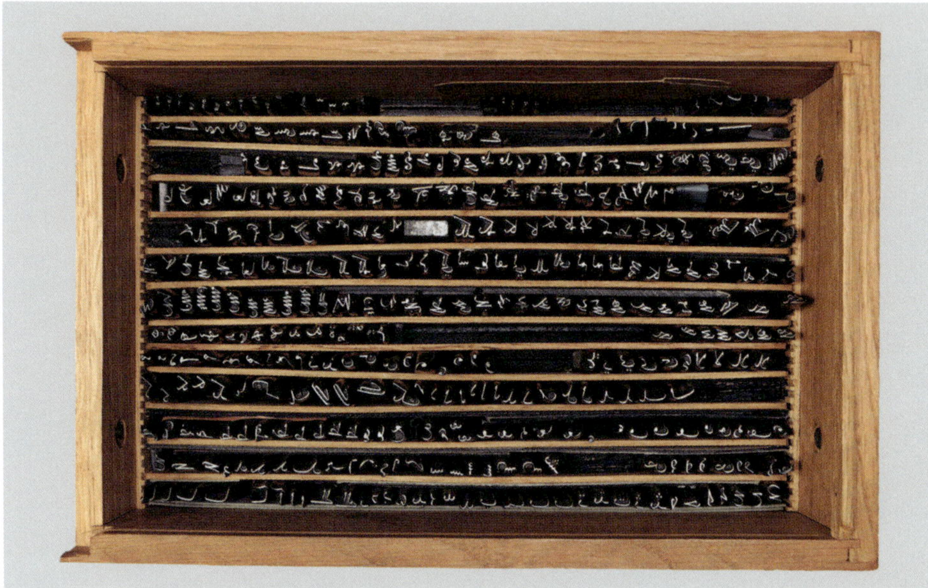

Fig. 1: Arabic types designed by Robert Granjon Fonds des Medici, 1590. Flers-en-Escrebieux France, Atelier du Livre d'art et de l'Estampe – Imprimerie nationale, inv. PO.IN.16

fifteenth century, in their printing. In the case of the first printed Qurʾān, these reasons were probably superseded by commercial interests. The first print was accomplished in Venice, Italy, in 1537–38, realized by Paganino and Alessandro Paganini, two major printers of the time. Only one copy of this Qurʾān, created by using wooden type, has been preserved and was discovered in 1987. Several studies have discussed this work, the incredible efforts to produce it, and the mistakes that made it unacceptable to Muslims. It appears this printing operation was launched with the desire to mount a business venture in the Ottoman Empire, with all the enthusiasm that characterizes the Venetian entrepreneurial world of that time. The high quality of the non-collated copy suggests that, rather than a production intended for wide circulation, it might have been destined for a client connected with the Ottoman court. Nevertheless, the poor quality of typographical characters and the printed text, resulting from imprecision in the production process and communication between the informants and the copy entrusted to the typographer, derailed the operation and forced the Paganinis into bankruptcy. Notwithstanding all this, such an enterprise remains an amazing attempt in terms of technical proficiency and entrepreneurial courage at the time.[1]

Before Paganini's time, a project possibly aimed at producing a printed edition of the Arabic Qurʾān together with a translation was sponsored by the humanist Cardinal Egidio da Viterbo (d.1532). However, the work did not have a wide circulation and only a couple of incomplete manuscripts survive. It remains unclear whether there were plans for a printed edition. At the time in the 1510s, there had been only a few attempts to print in Arabic, and manuscript distribution was still a prominent way to copy and disseminate such works.

After Paganini's failed enterprise, other scholars expressed their desire to edit and print the Qurʾān, although we often do not know whether they just wanted to manifest their proficiency in Arabic and the Qurʾān. These efforts resulted in a series of failed aspirations and only partial editions of Qurʾānic prints, as the European scholars working on these Arabic Qurʾān editions were facing significant challenges, including warfare, plagues, lack of economic support, and difficulties in finding or producing suitable Arabic types (**fig. 1**). Although several European scholars of Arabic and Islam were claiming to prepare a translation and edition of an Arabic Qurʾān in the second part of the sixteenth and seventeenth century, no such edition ever saw the light of day.

Franciscus Raphelengius (d.1597), for instance, is said to have engaged in a translation of the Qurʾān and also worked on printing an Arabic edition of the Qurʾān (**fig. 2**).[2] Thomas Erpenius (d.1624) promised in the preface to his edition and translation of Sura 12, *Surat Yusuf (Historia Josephi Patriarchae*, 1617) to produce a critical edition of the entire Arabic Qurʾān with a Latin translation. Christian Ravius (d.1677) and Jacob Golius (d.1667) also expressed their intentions to produce interlinear editions of the Qurʾān. Only very partial results materialised: Ravius edited the Arabic text and translated the first two suras in his *Prima tredecim partium Alcorani* from 1646. Unable to secure Arabic types, he printed the Arabic text in Hebrew translation, and employed a unique system of transcribing the Arabic text by means of Latin and Greek letters.

We now know that the same interest also prompted Arabic Qurʾān projects in seventeenth-century England, but nothing materialised.[3] The same is true of Germany, which Alastair Hamilton extensively discussed with regard to attempts of publishing an edition and new translation of the Qurʾān.[4] Here, the various publication endeavours were fuelled by the circulation of hundreds of Islamic manuscripts looted from Ottoman Europe in the years after the 1683 Siege of Vienna. Matthias Friedrich Beck (d.1701), Johann Andreas Danz (d.1727), and

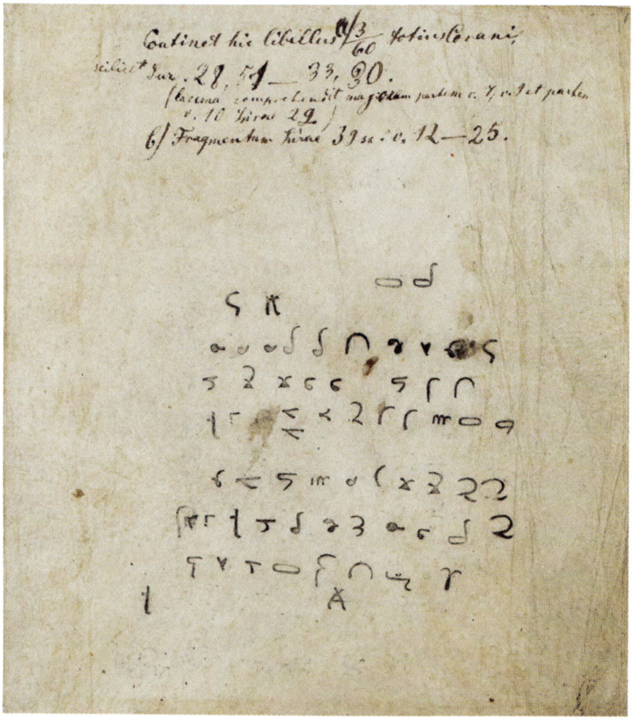

Fig. 2: Smoke proof on a Raphelengius manuscript from Tunis. Leiden University Libraries, Ms Or 251, fol. 1v

Sebastian Gottfried Starcke (d.1710) produced Latin specimens of individual suras (*Specimen arabicum*, 1688; *Specimen Alcorani Arabico-Latini*, 1690; *Specimen Versionis Coranicae*, 1698). Theodor Hackspan (d.1659) and Johann Georg Nissel (d.1662) also worked on such specimens, while Andreas Acolutus (d.1704), in his *Tetrapla Alcoranico, sive Specimen Alcorani quadrilinguis* (Berlin, 1701) edited and published an Arabic version of the text of Sura *al-Fatiha* together with a Persian and a Turkish translation as well as three separate Latin translations.[5] The most significant work on the Qurʾān prior to the late seventeenth century was done by Johann Zechendorff (1580–1662), who published two booklets on the Qurʾān and left a complete Arabic text together with a Latin interlinear translation of the whole Qurʾān in manuscript (**fig. 3**). Due to the Thirty Years' War and difficult post-war conditions in Central Europe, Zechendorff claimed to lack the financial resources and Arabic types to have his text and translation of the Qurʾān printed.[6]

This struggle to procure Arabic types was a constant concern in the testimonies of the Europeans who, after the Paganini edition, sought to edit and print an Arabic Qurʾān. In Italy, before the work of Ludovico Marracci, we know that Giovanni Battista Raimondi (d.1614), the editor of the Arabic texts published by Typographia Medicea, had also planned an edition of the Qurʾān. However, Typographia Medicea never published any Islamic religious work. Sara Fani's recent research demonstrates that Raimondi was certainly interested in the Qurʾān but did not go any further than some notes and first steps in the project.[7] The Jesuit Ignazio Lomellini (d.1645) also left a complete translation, together with the Arabic text and a polemical commentary in manuscript, possibly with plans to print it. Only one autograph copy has been preserved and undoubtedly deserves more attention.[8]

Fuelling Catholic and Protestant competition throughout the seventeenth century, ambitions to publish an Arabic Qurʾān were finally realized with two editions that appeared almost at the same time: one by Abraham Hinckelmann (d.1695) in Hamburg 1694 (**fig. 4**) and the other by Ludovico Marracci in Padua 1698 (**fig. 5**). Both editions were bold undertakings, intended for a small circle of Arabic experts and those proficient in oriental languages. Hinckelmann had planned to publish an edition together with a translation, but never accomplished the latter. Still, the Arabic text was spaced to provide ample room for notes and was often annotated by learners of Arabic. Marracci produced a monumental work with the Arabic text, a groundbreaking Latin translation, and quotations from Islamic commentary literature for each chapter of the Qurʾān, alternating between Arabic and Latin. Both editions show certain limitations in terms of the quality of typographic reproduction. Hinckelmann's and Marraci's was still a period of limited technical possibilities, and this was also one of the factors that caused the Ottoman printing religious texts with movable type during a period of ferocious opposition between the two shores of the Mediterranean.[9]

The last great European edition, published by Gustav Flügel (d.1870) in 1834, shared many of the same characteristics (**fig. 6**). The Arabic text had been improved but still could not keep up with the market's best calligraphic productions. In addition, eclectic choices had been made for the presentation of the text, which rendered it a problematic product in the eyes of Muslims. Notwithstanding these features and problems, Flügel's edition was reprinted several times (1841, 1855, 1867, 1870, 1881, 1893) and remained a reference work in Western studies on Islam until the mid-twentieth century. The sources used for the editions by

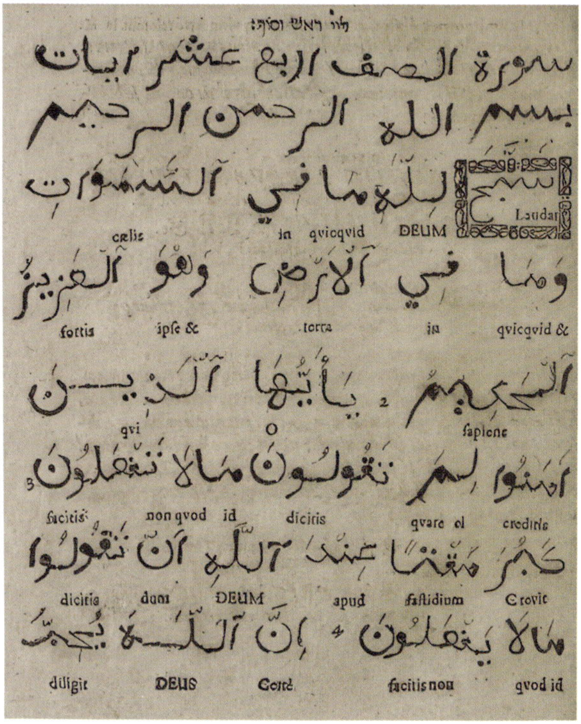

Fig. 3: Johann Zechendorff, *Specimen Suratarum id est, aliquote de Capitum ex Alcorani* (Zwickau, 1638), sig. 3v

Hinckelmann, Marracci, and Flügel, as well as the choices made by the editors are anything but straightforward. All these editions share a problematic relation to Muslim exegetical tradition: they display limited knowledge of the formal devices of Qurʾānic manuscripts, and generally convey the limits and problems connected to Arabic typographical products.

Printing the Qurʾān in the Muslim world

When Flügel published his edition in the early 1800s, both Muslim and non-Muslim printers had already begun printing books for the Islamic world. After an initial imperial initiative by the Russian Tsarina Catherine the Great (d.1796), who printed the sacred text for her Russian Muslim subjects in Saint Petersburg in 1787, various other editions followed in subsequent years. This resulted in the dissemination of a printed form of the Qurʾānic text that reflected Islamic

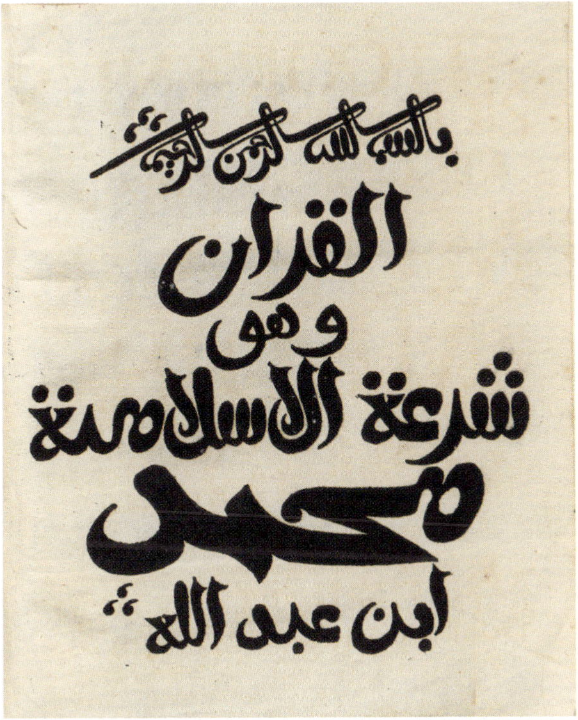

Fig. 4: Abraham Hinckelmann, *Alcoranus s. lex Islamitica Muhammedis* (Hamburg, 1694), title page

insight and stylistic features. Catherine's interest in printing and distributing the Qurʾān formed part of her inclusive policy towards Muslims. The edition was prepared for publication under the supervision of a *mullā* and was printed with Arabic types that had been created especially for the project. In 1801/02 at the request of the Kazan Tatars, the Arabic typeface of the St Petersburg Press was transferred to Kazan, where the Asiatic Press had been established at a local gymnasium a year before. As it was not permitted to publish Islamic religious literature in Saint Petersburg, numerous subsequent editions of the Qurʾān were printed in Kazan throughout the first half of the nineteenth century. These Qurʾāns printed in Kazan played a fundamental role in consolidating the dissemination of a particular reading of the Qurʾān (that by Ḥafṣ) not only among Islamic populations under Russian rule and in Central Asia, but also in the rest of the Islamic world, where they began to circulate in the nineteenth century.[10]

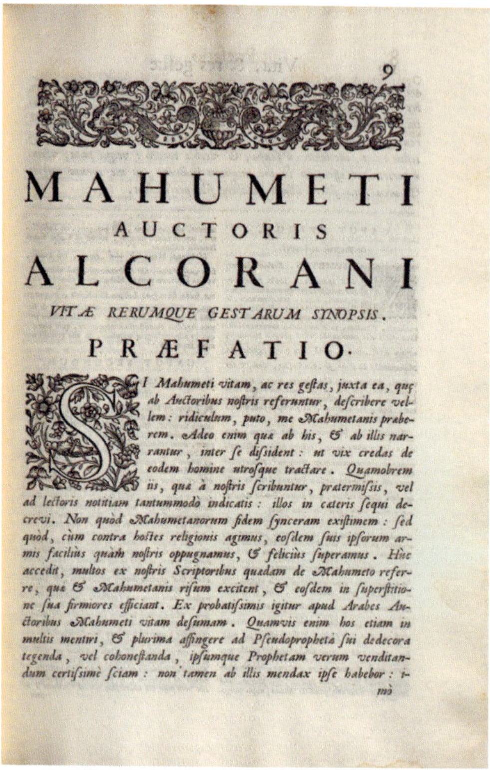

9

MAHUMETI
AUCTORIS
ALCORANI
VITÆ RERUMQUE GESTARUM SYNOPSIS.

PRÆFATIO.

SI Mahumeti vitam, ac res gestas, juxta ea, quę ab Auctoribus nostris referuntur, describere vellem: ridiculum, puto, me Mahumetanis praberem. Adeo enim qua ab his, & ab illis narrantur, inter se dissident: ut vix credas de eodem homine utrosque tractare. Quamobrem iis, qua à nostris scribuntur, pratermissis, vel ad lectoris notitiam tantummodò indicatis: illos in cateris sequi decrevi. Non quòd Mahumetanorum fidem synceram existimem: sed quòd, cùm contra hostes religionis agimus, eosdem suis ipsorum armis faciliùs quàm nostris oppugnamus, & feliciùs superamus. Hùc accedit, multos ex nostris Scriptoribus quadam de Mahumeto referre, qua & Mahumetanis risum excitent, & eosdem in superstitione sua firmiores efficiant. Ex probatissimis igitur apud Arabes Auctoribus Mahumeti vitam desumam. Quamvis enim hos etiam in multis mentiri, & plurima affingere ad Pseudopropheta sui dedecora tegenda, vel cohonestanda, ipsumque Prophetam verum venditandum certissimè sciam: non tamen ab illis mendax ipse habebor: imò

Fig. 5: Ludovico Marracci, *Alcorani textus universus* (Padua, 1698), vol. 1, 9

In addition to the possibility of spreading the text across areas of relative or reduced literacy, it was probably the sheer volume of these editions that caused the production of printed Qur'āns to jump to other Muslim regions. Russia, India, and Iran were the first nations to produce printed Qur'āns, generally in a lithographic form that guaranteed more control over the layout of the page, with an appearance that more closely resembled manuscript copies. Moreover, the Ottoman Empire had long-lasting trade and diplomatic networks with Europe, where the print revolution had already begun in the mid-fifteenth century. Ottoman bans and a general disinterest in the new printing technology stalled any printing progress until the nineteenth century, when copies of the Qur'ān printed in India, Russia, and Iran began to enter and change

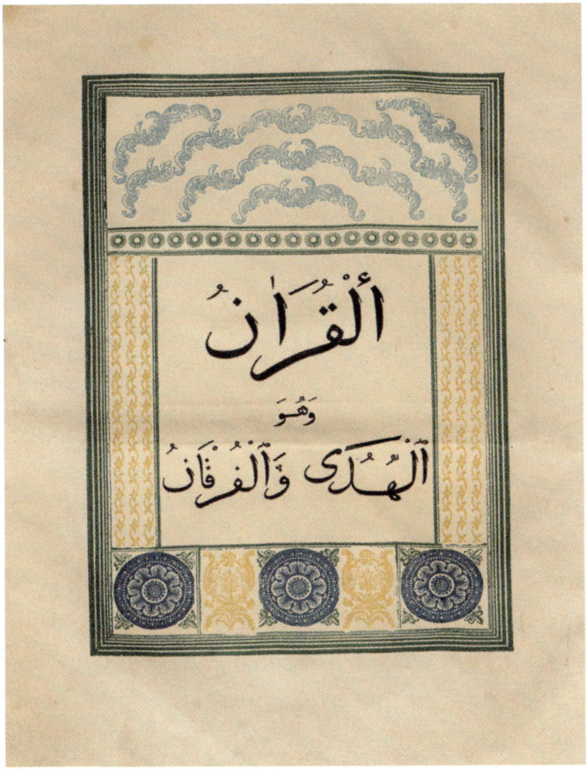
القرآن
وهو
الهدى والفرقان

Fig. 6: Gustav Flügel, *Corani textus arabicus* (Leipzig, 1834), title page

the Ottoman Empire. As a result, we see a first attempt to produce a printed Qurʾān in Istanbul in 1856. Commercial interests and the benefits of large-scale, controlled dissemination of the text inevitably prevailed over resistance from scribal guilds, religious doubts regarding issues of purity, and the reluctance caused by the greater aesthetic quality of manuscript copies.[11]

Between the late nineteenth and early twentieth century, the printing of Qurʾāns spread over various regions of the Islamic world, following the pattern of other book genres, which revolutionized people's access to intellectual production, and opened the entire Islamic world to a culture that was no longer dependent on manuscript transmission. Together with India and Iran, Egypt quickly emerged as one of the most important actors in the production of books with movable types, including the Qurʾān. Egypt took the next big step in the printing of the Qurʾān: the progressive homogenization of the published form in the famous edition of 1924. Named in honour of King Fu'ād of Egypt, the historical development of this edition was similar to those giving rise to the definitive dissemination of printing.

This version, not free from criticism, was the object of later revisions, especially from 1936, known as the Fārūq edition, named after the ruling Egyptian king at the time. While specifically created for educational purposes, the Cairo edition and its successive revisions became a point of reference for nearly all subsequent editions. Despite revisions and differences that highlighted a continual process of adaptation, this development rendered the version of Ḥafṣ to become the dominant form of the Qurʾān in the entire world.[12]

The later success of printed editions is marked by the increasing importance of the reading of Ḥafṣ via ʿĀṣim, and by the use of the 1924 Cairo edition and later editions as the basis for modifications and improvements, though in a limited and gradual manner. In recent decades, the most active agents in this endeavour have been Saudi Arabia and the Gulf countries, which have been continuously funding the production of printed Qurʾāns and promoting a certain form of the text. The foundation of official institutions, starting with the Qurʾān printing agency, created by al-Azhar in 1977, and the organization named after King Fahd, established in Saudi Arabia in 1985, paved the way for investing significant resources into the dissemination of the Qurʾān in various print editions in an age when various media introduced new ways of spreading the Holy Qurʾān.

1 See Angela M. Nuovo, *Alessandro Paganini* (1509–38) (Padua, 1990); Maurice Borrmans, 'Observations à propos de la première édition imprimée du Coran à Venise,' *Quaderni di Studi Arabi* 8 (1990): 3–12; Maurice Borrmans, 'Présentation de la première édition du Coran à Venise,' *Quaderni di Studi Arabi* 9 (1991): 93–126; Hartmut Bobzin, *Ließ ein Papst den Koran verbrennen?: Mutmaßungen zum Venezianer Korandruck von 1537/38; vorgetragen in der Sitzung vom 10. Dezember 2004* (Munich, 2013).

2 Alastair Hamilton, '"Nam tirones sumus" Franciscus Raphelengius' Lexicon Arabico-Latinum (Leiden, 1613)', in Marcus de Schepper et al. (eds.), *Ex Officina Plantiniana. Studia in memoriam Christophori Plantini (c.1520–1589)* (Antwerpen, 1989), 557–89.

3 Nabil Matar, *Islam in Britain 1558–1685* (Cambridge, 1998), 74–5 on the difficulties of printing the Qurʾān.

4 Alastair Hamilton, '"To Rescue the Honour of the Germans": Qurʾān translations by eighteenth- and early nineteenth-century

German protestants', *Journal of the Warburg and Courtauld Institutes*, 77 (2014), 173–209; ibid., 'A Lutheran translator for the Qur'ān. A late seventeenth-century quest', in A. Hamilton, M.H. van den Boogert, and B. Westerwell, (eds.), *The Republic of Letters and the Levant* (Leiden and Boston, 2005), 197–221.

5 See, in particular, Hamilton 2005 (see note 4), 209–12; Hartmut Bobzin, 'Die Koranpolyglotte des Andreas Acoluthus (1654–1704)', in *Germano-Turcica. Zur Geschichte des Türkisch-Lernens in den deutschsprachigen Ländern* (Bamberg, 1987), 57–9; Hartmut Bobzin, 'Latin Translations of the Koran. A short overview', *Der Islam*, 70 (1993), 193–206.

6 See Roberto Tottoli, 'The Latin translation of the Qur'ān by Johann Zechendorff (1580–1662) discovered in Cairo Dār al-Kutub', *Oriente Moderno*, 95 (2015), 5–31; Reinhold Glei, 'A presumed lost Latin translation of the Qur'ān (Johann Zechendorff, 1632)', *Neulateinisches Jahrbuch. Journal of Neo-Latin Language and Literature*, 18 (2016) 361–72.

7 Sara Fani, 'Printing the Qur'ān in Rome: From the Typographia Medicea to Marracci's Paduan edition', in Federico Stella and Roberto Tottoli (eds.), *The Qur'ān in Rome. Manuscripts, Translations, and the Study of Islam in Early Modern Catholicism* (Berlin and Boston 2024), 79–122, in particular 93–102.

8 See on this work Paul Shore, *A Baroque Jesuit's Encounter with the Qur'ān. An Examination of Ignazio Lomellini's, S. J., Animadversiones, Notae ac Disputationes in Pestilentem Alcoranum* (Wiesbaden, 2023).

9 On Marracci's work, see Reinhold Glei and Roberto Tottoli, *Ludovico Marracci at Work: The Evolution of His Latin Translation of the Qur'ān in the Light of His Newly Discovered Manuscripts with an Edition and a Comparative Linguistic Analysis of Sura* 18 (Wiesbaden, 2016); Roberto Tottoli, 'New Light on the Translation of the Qur'ān of Ludovico Marracci from His Manuscripts Recently Discovered at the Order of the Mother of God in Rome,' in Andrew Rippin and Roberto Tottoli (eds.), *Books and Written Culture of Islamic World.Studies Presented to Claude Gilliot on the Occasion of His 75th Birthday* (Leiden and Boston, 2015), 91–130. On Hinckelmann, see Hellmut Braun, 'Der Hamburger Koran von 1694,' in Christian Voigt and Erich Zimmermann (eds.), *Libris et Litteris. Festschrift für H. Tiemann zum sechzigsten Geburtstag am 9. Juli 1959* (Hamburg, 1959), 149–66.

10 Efim A. Rezvan, 'The Qur'ān and Its World: VI. Emergence of the Canon: The Struggle for Uniformity,' *Manuscripta Orientalia* 4/2 (1998), 26; Efim A. Rezvan, 'The Qur'ān and Its World: VIII/2. *West-östliche Divans* (The Qur'ān in Russia),' *Manuscripta Orientalia* 5/1 (1999), 36–40.

11 Brett M. Wilson, *Translating the Qur'ān in an Age of Nationalism. Print Culture and Modern Islam in Turkey* (London, Oxford, 2014), 55–83. On the 1918 edition and the informative appendices of the 1924 edition, see Muhammad A. Abdel Haleem, 'Qur'ānic Orthography. The Written Representation of the Recited Text of the Qur'ān,' *Islamic Quarterly* 34 (1994): 180–7. On the editions of the Qur'ān printed in London in the nineteenth century for various purposes, see Michael W. Albin, 'Printing of the Qur'ān,' *Encyclopaedia of the Qur'ān* (Leiden – Boston, 2004), 4:265.

12 'Abd al-Fattāḥ al-Qāḍī, *al-Muṣḥaf ash-sharīf: Abḥāth fī tārīkhihi wa-aḥkāmihi* (Cairo, 1388/1968); Abū al-Futūḥ Riḍwān, *Tārīkh maṭba'at Būlāq wa-lamḥa fī tārīkh aṭ-ṭibā'a fī buldān ash-Sharq al-Awsaṭ* (Cairo, 1953); Gotthelf Bergsträsser, 'Koranlesung in Kairo. I,' *Der Islam* 20 (1932), 2–13. See also Albin 2004 (see note 11), 272; Natalia K. Suit, 'Qur'ānic Matters: Media and Materiality' (PhD diss., University of North Carolina, Chapel Hill, 2014); Wilson, *Translating the Qur'ān in an Age of Nationalism*, 189–190. See also Adrian Brockett, 'Studies in Two Transmissions of the Qur'ān' (PhD diss., University of St. Andrews, 1984), on the differences between the diverse editions of the twentieth century of the Qur'ān according to Ḥafṣ.

The Qurʾān and European Literature: a Romantic Discovery

Emmanuelle Stefanidis, University of Nantes

In 1697, a few years before his bestselling adaptation of *One Thousand and One Nights* captivated the literary imagination of his time, the scholar of oriental languages Antoine Galland (1646–1715) pondered over the significance of the Qurʾān for Christian European readers. What should we make of the Qurʾān's 'fanciful' retellings of Biblical narratives? Breaking with centuries of polemical engagement with the Muslim Scripture, Galland underlined the pleasure one derives from reading the Qurʾān: 'Whether these traditions are false or whether they are true, it is always very pleasing to know them.'[1] By extracting the Qurʾān from the test of truth – a radical move in the deeply Catholic context of his times – Galland's statement anticipates the literary curiosity for the Sacred Scripture of Islam in the post-Enlightenment age.

The eighteenth-century public appreciation of the Qurʾān's aesthetic dimension in Galland's comments was a novel phenomenon in literary circles. From a Christian apologetic standpoint, any consideration of the stylistic beauty of the Muslim Scripture amounted to excessive praise for a rival and feared religion. The appreciation of Qurʾānic beauty had, moreover, important theological ramifications. In the Islamic tradition, the Qurʾān's poetic qualities were considered the greatest proof of its miraculous nature. The doctrine of the 'inimitability' of

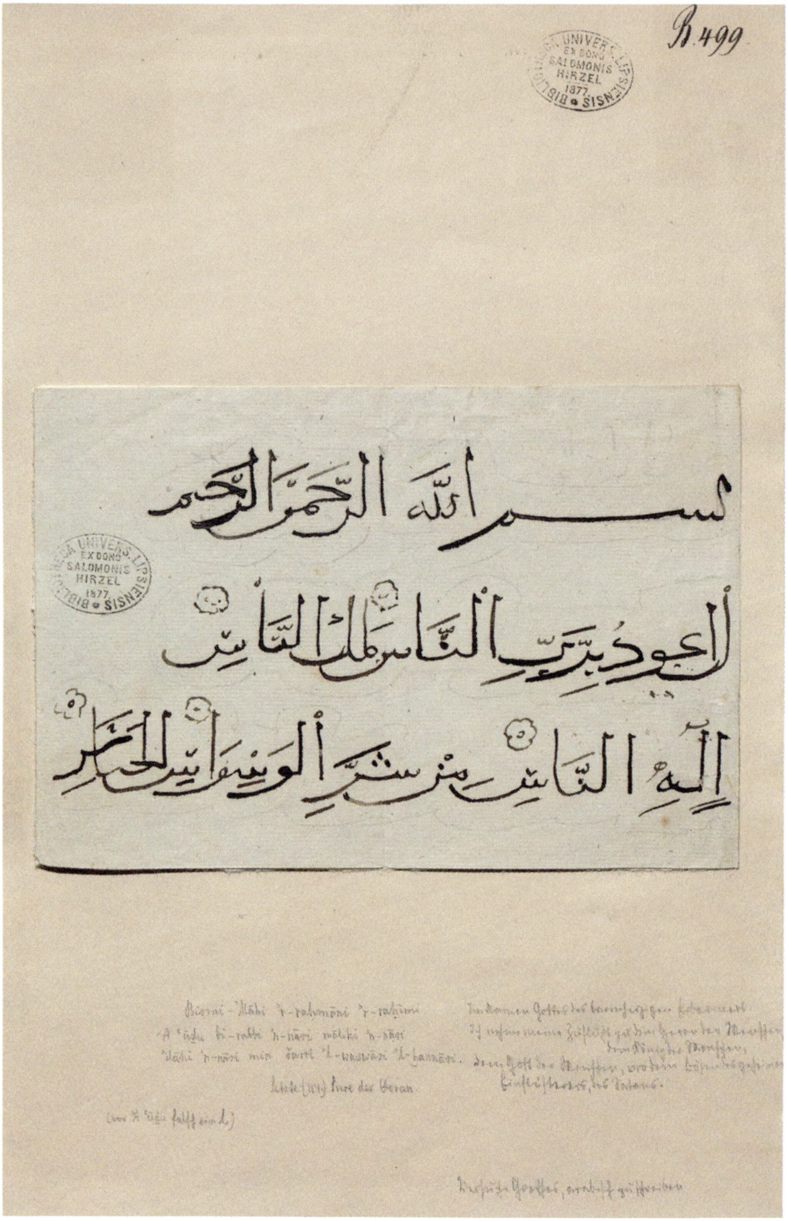

Fig. 1: Goethe's attempt to copy Sura 114 (*an-nas*).
Universitätsbibliothek Leipzig, Hirzel B 499, fol. 1r.

the Qurʾān (*iʿjāz al-Qurʾān*) – as it came to be known – is rooted in the challenge the Qurʾān addresses to its detractors to produce a discourse of equal poetic force.[2] Christian European authors had been aware of the doctrine of *iʿjāz* since at least the thirteenth century. Many were consequently wary of praising the aesthetic qualities of the Muslim Scripture. There are occasional brief references to the 'elegance' of the Qurʾān in the writings of scholars such as Nicolas of Cusa (1401–64), Claude Duret (1570–1611), and Henry Stubbe (1631–76). Most authors, however, emphasized the Qurʾān's absence of order and its alleged confusion – the 'Alcoran chaos', as one author put it.[3] The 'disordered' nature of the Qurʾān constituted a polemical trope in Christian anti-Muslim apologetics that can be traced back to the first Latin translation of the Qurʾān commissioned by Abbott Peter of Cluny in the 1140s. Reduced to a hodgepodge of Christian and Jewish traditions, the Qurʾān's 'disjointed' structure was cited by polemicists as evidence of its heretical origin and forged character. The dominance of religious polemics limited the scope for any poetic exploration of the Qurʾān during much of the history of Christian-Muslim interaction.

The public's perception of Islam started to change in the second half of the seventeenth century due to a convergence of political, scholarly, and cultural factors. The end of the 'Turkish Menace', symbolized by the failed Siege of Vienna in 1683, gave way to normalized relations between Christian powers and the Ottomans. Wider access to Arabic, Turkish, and Persian manuscripts provided scholars of oriental languages with more accurate and increasingly specialized knowledge of the Orient. The loosening of the Christian grip in the wake of Enlightenment opened up some space for sympathetic approaches to Islam. Timely concerns with political governance allowed for novel appraisals of Muhammad as a reformer, lawgiver, and statesman, while the doctrine of Deism, popular among philosophers, was projected onto Islam's 'purified' monotheism.

Scholarly and philosophical approaches to Islam laid the groundwork for a literary appreciation of the Muslim Scripture which took off in the Romantic era. The Qurʾān attracted some of the greatest Romantic authors of the nineteenth century, chief among them Johann Wolfgang von Goethe (1749–1832; see **fig. 1**), Alexander Pushkin (1799–1837), and Victor Hugo (1802–85). Their engagement with the Qurʾān inspired later authors, effectively integrating the Muslim Scripture into the European literary canon. The Romantics' interest in Muhammad's proclamations was shaped by the movement's exploration of poetic inspiration and the relations between language, mythology, and culture. Four aspects of the Muslim Scripture made it particularly relevant to Romantic sensitivity: the Qur'ān's oriental origin, its style and content, revelatory status, and civilizational impact. Let us look at each of these aspects in turn, showing how the Romantics drew on, and reformulated, European scholarly and literary perspectives on Islam.

The Qur'ān and the Orient

Ever since the Middle Ages, the 'Orient' had been a source of conflicting attitudes and attachments in the European imagination. It had assumed the role, all at once, of the mythical Holy Land, a well-trodden pilgrimage site, the realm of Saracens and later Turks, and the scene of the Crusades. With the dissemination of Galland's hugely successful adaptation of *Arabian Nights*, the Orient also became the land of fairy tales, magic, and exoticism. The oriental tale entered the literary canon, turning into a versatile genre of entertainment, creative output, philosophical inquiry, and social critique. Examples include Pétis de la Croix's *Mille et un Jours* (1710–12), Montesquieu's *Lettres Persanes* (1721), Voltaire's *Zadig* (1748), and William Beckford's *Vathek* (1782).

In the second half of the eighteenth century, Germans discovered the intricate tradition of ancient Arabic poetry and the world of nomadic Arabs. Johann Jacob Reiske (1716–74) first published a translation of one of the foundational Arabic odes, the *Mu'allaqa of Tarfa*, in 1742, a few years before his peer and scholarly rival, Johann David Michaelis (1717–91), wrote a laudatory treaty on oriental poetry (*Von dem Geschmack der morgenländischen Dichtkunst*, 1752). William Jones's translation of the seven *Mu'allaqat* in 1783 had the greatest literary impact. Translated into German by Anton Theodor Hartmann under the evocative title *Die hellstrahlenden Plejaden am arabischen poetischen Himmel* ('The Luminous Pleiades in the Arabic Poetic Sky', 1802), Jones's work became a source of inspiration for Goethe's famous *West-östlicher Divan* (1819) and Victor Hugo's *Les Orientales* (1829).

The discovery of pre-Islamic poetry changed the perception of the Qur'ān in two ways. First, it allowed Europeans to situate the Muslim Scripture in a sophisticated literary tradition. The Qur'ān was more than a 'jumble' of Christian and Jewish heresies; it carried its own poetic force. Secondly, Arabic poetry was presented by Reiske, Michaelis, and Jones as replete with strong emotions, honour, courage, adventure, and the love of freedom. This description appealed to the Romantics, who hoped to revive Western thought and values, shackled by rationalist thought, through oriental passion. The promises and fantasies of the Orient were constitutive of the Romantic movement in its varied national settings. As an exotic, mysterious, and evocative site, the Orient provided an endless resource to the literary imagination. 'My head is full of oriental names and scenes', commented the English poet Lord Byron (1788–1824) in a private letter, dated of 1813, as he was writing his *Eastern Tales*.

Given the Romantic fascination with the Orient, their interest in the Qurʾān as the foundational text of Muslim civilization was unavoidable. Many poets read it, though only a few ended up citing it in their literary production. Byron describes the *Koran* in his reading notes as a text that 'contains most sublime poetical passages, far surpassing European poetry.' As a teenager, Rimbaud (1854–91) read a French translation of the Qurʾān found in his father's library. The direct influence of the Qurʾān on his poetry is limited to a few echoes of paradisaical descriptions. Rimbaud's interest in the Muslim Scripture resurfaced later in life when, having turned away from poetry, Rimbaud worked as a tradesman in Abyssinia. He roamed the Horn of Africa with a lithograph edition of the Qurʾān in his luggage, which he had learned to read in the original language.

The Qurʾān was also perceived as a gateway to the Biblical world due to its textual and geographical proximity to the Old and New Testament. It was believed that the world of the Arabs, in the harsh desert of Arabia, shared characteristics with that of the Biblical patriarchs and the Christian desert fathers. In 1846, Gustave Flaubert (1821–80) took copious notes of the Qurʾān in preparation for an 'oriental tale': 'I search for colour, poetry, sound, warmth and beauty,' he explained in a private letter dated from September 1846. His *Conte Oriental* was never completed, but the preparatory work was eventually incorporated into *La tentation de Saint Antoine* (1874), depicting the inner turmoil of the third-century hermit.

The style and content of the Qurʾān

Romantic poetry favoured the expression of strong emotions, mystical aspirations, and awe for the natural world, all of which are found in abundance in the Qurʾān. Many Europeans reading the Qurʾān discovered a form and content pleasing to their aesthetic tastes. They were able to rely on Enlightenment translations of the Qurʾān, which refrained from derogatory remarks and attempted to convey the elevated rhetoric of the Muslim Scripture. George Sale's English rendition of the Qurʾān (1734) was pioneering in this regard. In a context still infused with religious hostility, Sale underlined that the Qurʾānic style was 'generally beautiful and fluent'. Largely devoid of polemical intent, Sale's translation was instrumental in making the Qurʾān accessible for literary and philosophical purposes. Sale's 'very beautiful' translation led Voltaire (1694–1778) to revise his attitude towards Islam and its Prophet.[4] As a staunch rationalist, Voltaire was not prone to value the passionate and mystical flights of the Qurʾān. In his *Dictionnaire philosophique* (1764), Voltaire had characterised the Qurʾān as 'a rhapsody without connection, order or art.' Yet, in a revised edition of the *Essai sur les Moeurs* (1775), the emblematic philosopher of the Lumières encouraged his readers to 'read the beginning of the Koran, it is sublime.'

The impact of Sale's translation of the Qurʾān rippled beyond the English readership. Goethe first encountered the Qurʾān in 1771, at the age of twenty-two, through Theodor Arnold's German translation of Sale's work (1746). As a young author, Goethe was deeply impressed by the poetic and prophetic drive of Muhammad's revelations. In a letter to his mentor Johann Gottfried von Herder (1744–1803), he expressed his writer's anguish using Qurʾānic imagery: 'I would like to pray like Moses in the Qurʾān: Lord, open up my breast' (July 1772). As a challenging text, the Qurʾān did not captivate all Romantic authors. Thomas Carlyle (1795–1881), whose opinion of the Prophet was highly positive, famously decried the Scripture of Islam as 'a wearisome, confused jumble' (1841). The Qurʾān left few readers indifferent. As Goethe put it, '[w]henever we turn to it, [the Qurʾān] always freshly repels us, but then once again draws us to it, arouses amazement and in the end demands reverence.' Goethe defined the Qurʾānic style as 'strong, great, frightening, in passages truly sublime (*erhaben*).'[5] The adjective 'sublime' is repeatedly used in the nineteenth century to characterise both the style and content of the Qurʾān. The term goes back to Greco-Roman attempts to theorize literary and rhetorical power. Its application, however, was expanded in the Romantic period to define an awe-inspiring encounter with the unfathomable, beyond human rationality. Romantic poetry, like the short-lived *Sturm und Drang* period that preceded it, valued sublimity most highly.

An eighteenth-century German translation of the Qurʾān illustrates the growing appeal of the Muslim Scripture's style and content for European readers. Forty years after Sale's translation, a student of the renowned scholar of oriental languages Christian Benedikt Michaelis, Friedrich Eberhard Boysen (1720–1800), sought to convey the 'splendour of Muhammad's muse'. Boysen felt humbled by the daunting task. In a 1745 letter to his friend, the poet Ludwig Gleim (1719–1803), Boysen lamented: 'I would need your spirit if I wanted to translate the Koran; there is so much fire and majesty in this poem!'[6] His translation eventually appeared in 1773. Two years later, in a revised edition, Boysen expressed admiration for Muhammad. Although his defence of the Prophet was

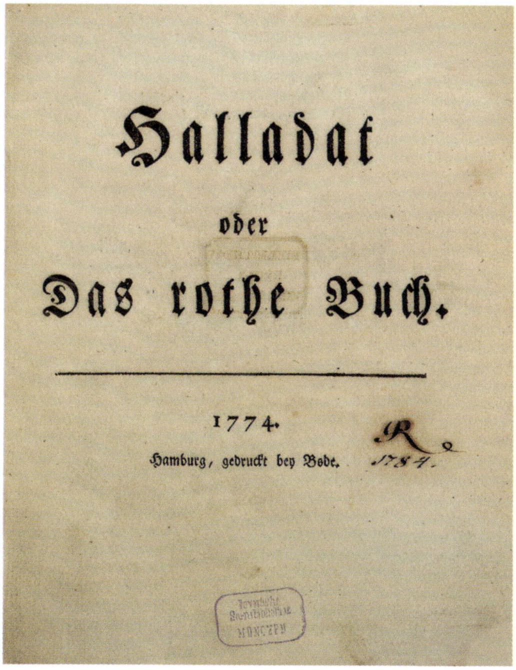

Fig. 2: Johann Wilhelm Ludwig Gleim, *Halladat oder das Rothe Buch* (Vienna, 1774), title page

deplored, the aesthetic ambitions of his translation were well-received. Even so, Gleim wished his friend had gone further in his poetic rendition of the Qurʾān. He regretted Boysen's decision to use prose, since the Qurʾān uses rhyme and assonance. Gleim embarked on a singular project to give a sense of the literary qualities of the Arabic version: to write his own Qurʾān in German. Entitled *Halladat, oder Das rothe Buch*, Gleim's 'Qurʾān' comprised thirty-one poems depicting man's relationship to his creator, to his fellow humans, and to nature (**fig. 2**). The term *Halladat* was one of Gleim's orientalizing inventions. He defined it as a 'red book' in which 'the wise man writes down his best and freest thoughts.' Appearing anonymously in 1774, *Halladat* was the first of a series of poetic engagements with the Qurʾān. Boysen included two of Gleim's poems in the preface of his translation. Referring to the source of these poems as 'a second Qurʾān' from a 'friend', Boysen hoped that these original 'suras' would offer German readers a taste of the poetic spirit of Arabic. Although a poetic

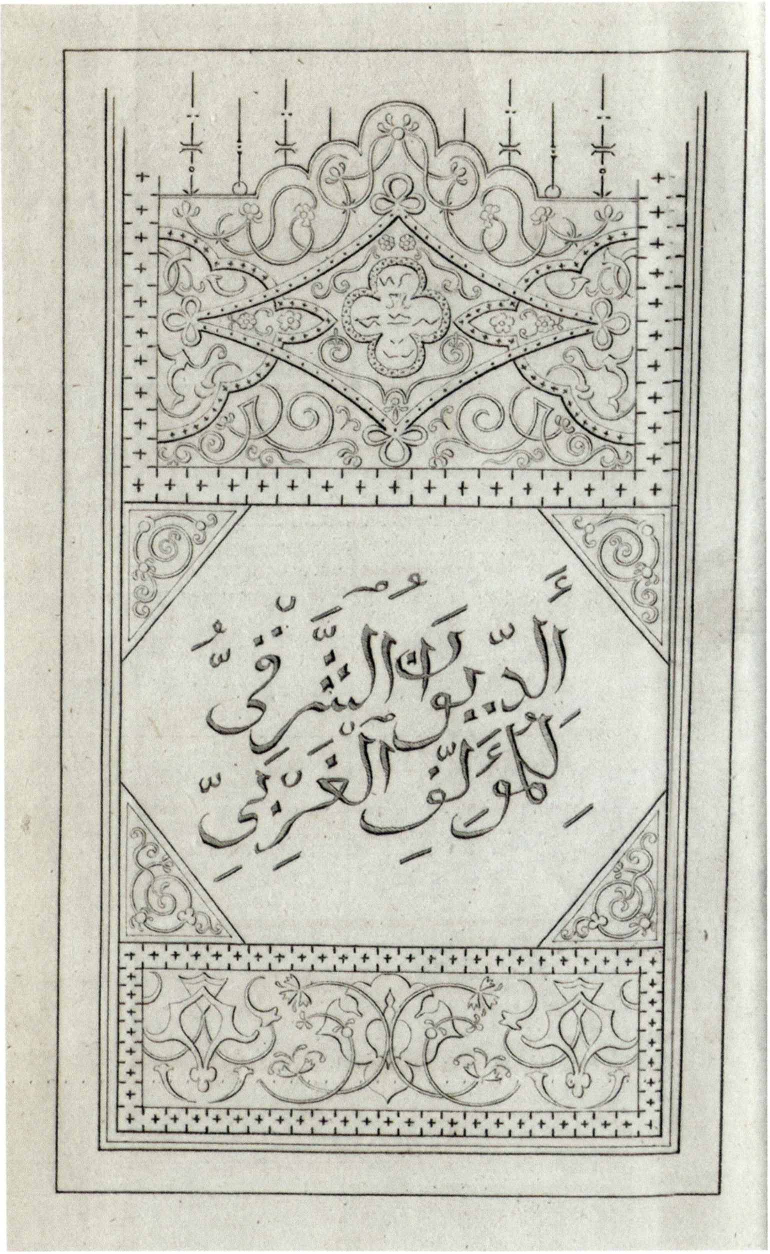

Fig. 3: Extract from Goethe's *West-Eastern Divan*, evocation of Q 2:142, 1819. Weimar, Goethe- und Schiller-Archiv, GSA 25/W 797, ornamental opening page

appreciation of the Qurʾān was starting to get a hold in proto-Romantic circles, Gleim's desire to remain anonymous reminds us that close engagements with the Qurʾān still remained controversial in the eighteenth century.

The Qurʾān's revelatory claims

A third aspect of the Qurʾān, which Romanticism invested with new meaning, was its revelatory claims. According to Muslim belief, Muhammad was a messenger and received his revelations from God through the Archangel Gabriel. Christian polemicists retorted that Muhammad was the author of the Qurʾān and that his claim of being a prophet was a clear indication of his imposture. Breaking from both traditions, the Romantics envisioned the Qurʾān's revelatory status through their own poetic-prophetic aspirations. Romanticism conceived gifted inspiration as an exterior force imposing itself on the poet. Reacting against the Enlightenment's excessive reliance on human reason, Romantics celebrated the human genius, able to communicate to fellow humans a glimpse of the divine truth hidden in nature. The blurring of the frontier between poetry and prophecy had a precedent in the study of the Bible. In 1741, the clergyman Robert Lowth gave a series of lectures on Hebrew poetry at the University of Oxford, where he put forward the category of sacred poetry primarily defined in terms of the 'sublime'. These lectures were collected and published first in Britain as *De Sacra Poesi Hebraeorum* (1753), and later in two instalments in Germany by Johann David Michaelis (1758, 1761). Michaelis's edition profoundly shaped the emerging *Sturm und Drang* poets.

The Qurʾān was not the Bible, of course; it was the controversial scripture of a competing religion. However, sacred poetry and the sublime provided a framework that could easily accommodate a sympathetic account of the Muslim account of revelation. The Austrian diplomat, orientalist scholar, and translator of a selection of suras (1811), Joseph von Hammer-Purgstall, acquiesced effortlessly in the Muslim doctrine that the Qurʾān 'could not have been the fruit of human inspiration: it must have been spoken and written in heaven from eternity', for '[o]nly the supreme magic of language could stamp the word of the son of Abdallah (i.e., Muhammad) as the word of God.'

Hammer-Purgstall was a prolific writer, translator, and cultural mediator, who introduced his readers to the rich repertoire of Persian poetry. His translation of the fourteenth-century Persian poet Hafez incited Goethe, then in his late sixties, to compose a hybrid work of poetry that had a momentous effect on European poetry: *The West-Eastern Divan*, which appeared in 1819 (**fig. 3**). This collection of more than two hundred poems – divided into twelve books, each prefaced with a Persian and a German title – represented a meeting of two cultures, orchestrated by the greatest German-speaking writer of his time. Goethe redrew the borders of German poetic tradition. He also redefined Islam for his European readership in a much-cited couplet: *Wenn Islam Gott ergeben heisst / Im Islam leben und sterben wir alle* ('If "Islam" signifies "submitting to God" / In Islam, we all live and die'). Verses from the Qurʾān are woven into the poetic matter of the *Divan* from its start. The fourth poem, entitled 'Talismans' (*Talismane*), declares, in an adaptation of verse 142 of the *Surat al-Baqara*, 'To God belongs the Orient! To God belongs the Occident!' The poem was put into music by Robert Schumann in 1840, reverberating Qurʾānic expressions into German high culture. The Qurʾān's revelatory status is the object of another poem in the *Divan*:

Ob der Koran von Ewigkeit sei?
Darnach frag' ich nicht!
Ob der Koran geschafen sei?
Das weiß ich nicht!
Daß er das Buch der Bücher sei
Glaub' ich aus Mosleminen-Plicht.

Is the Qurʾān from eternity?
That, I will not ask.
Might the Qurʾān created be?
No answer – a thankless task.
That it the Book of Books need be
My Muslim faith made clear to me.[7]

Goethe concludes the poem with a playfully irreverent ode to wine drinking, indicating that his declaration of Muslim faith was meant tongue-in-cheek. His characterization of the Qurʾān as the 'Book of Books' is nevertheless remarkable. The expression comes close to the Muslim notion of the 'Mother of the Book' (*umm al-kitāb*), the heavenly-guarded tablet, containing knowledge of past and future events from which the Qurʾān emanates.

The Qurʾān's civilisational impact

The Muslim account of the Qurʾān made it a book of truly epic proportions, which could not fail to impress Romantic authors, as they reflected on the power

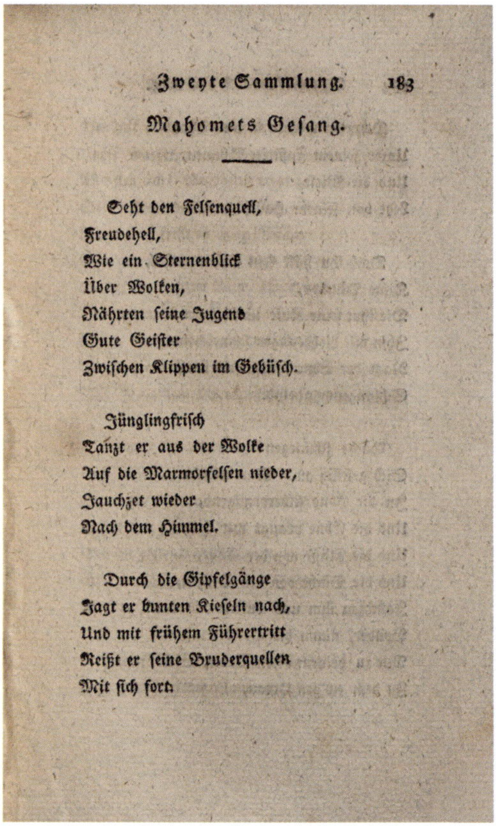

Zweyte Sammlung. 183

Mahomets Gesang.

Seht den Felsenquell,
Freudehell,
Wie ein Sternenblick
Über Wolken,
Nährten seine Jugend
Gute Geister
Zwischen Klippen im Gebüsch.

Jünglingfrisch
Tanzt er aus der Wolke
Auf die Marmorfelsen nieder,
Jauchzet wieder
Nach dem Himmel.

Durch die Gipfelgänge
Jagt er bunten Kieseln nach,
Und mit frühem Führertritt
Reißt er seine Bruderquellen
Mit sich fort.

Fig. 4: *Mahomets Gesang* ('Mahomet's Song'), in Goethe's *Schriften*, vol. 8 (Leipzig, 1789), 183

of literature to unite a people. Nationhood was the question of the day in the German lands. The intellectual dynamism of the *Aufklärung* placed German thought at Europe's centre stage at a time when the Holy Roman Empire had entered a period of political decline, eventually leading to its dissolution in 1806. Seeking to define German identity without the support of a centralized authority, thinkers located the nation's unity in a common language. Johann Gottfried von Herder, a major figure of the *Sturm und Drang* movement, theorised the role of literature as the most vivid expression of a folk's identity and genius. In his comparative study of poetry, he considered the poetic production of the Arabs alongside that of the Hebrews, Greeks, Romans, and Celts. He singled out the Qurʾān not only for its 'sublime' passages but also for its enduring effect on the cultural identity of the Arabs. '[P]oetry … is essentially effective,' writes Herder; '[i]t imprints itself on the soul just as a seal forms an image in wax or glue.'[8] Muhammad's 'masterpiece of poetry' (*Meisterstück von Dichtkunst*) was taken as a model. For Herder, the primary task of German literature was to produce a work of genius that united the German spirit, as Shakespeare's plays had achieved for the English a century earlier. Goethe would prove himself to be just such a genius, particularly through the publication of his *magnum opus, Faust* (1808, 1832).

As a Lutheran pastor, Herder oscillated between two understandings of Muhammad. At times, he considered the founder of Islam a cunning impostor; in other moments, he depicted the Muslim Prophet as a genius who successfully used poetry to advance his cause. Muhammad was, however, a compelling model for poets with national aspirations, such as Goethe, Pushkin, and Victor Hugo. Goethe expressed his admiration by composing a laudatory play on the Prophet, which he did not complete. Among the surviving fragments is a poem entitled *Mahomets Gesang* ('Mahomet's Song'), where Goethe described the Prophet's spirit and beneficent legacy in naturalistic terms, using the metaphor of a stream growing into a river, causing the valley to bloom, joyfully gathering each and all on the way to a mystical reunion with the Father (**fig. 4**).

A similar fascination with the Prophet and the Qurʾān can be found in Alexander Pushkin's work. An admirer of Goethe, Pushkin adhered to the Romantic concept of prophetic poetry. His celebrated poem *The Prophet* (1828), written in first person, depicts a dramatic divine calling through an Angel: 'Arise, prophet, and see and understand, Become filled with my will, And as you traverse seas and lands, Scorch the hearts of people with your tongue.' Pushkin's readers understood the poem as a reference to Isaiah's calling in the Bible. However, the Angelic mediation and the motif of the splitting of the chest ('he cleaved my chest with a sword and removed the trembling heart'[9]) point to a Muhammadan model. The opening of the Prophet's chest is a famous episode of Muhammad's hagiography, in which the angels purify his heart in preparation for his mission. The event, which had already inspired the young Goethe, is mentioned in Sura 94 of the Qurʾān known as 'The Expansion [of the breast]'. Beyond the Biblical and Qurʾānic referent, it was understood that the great Russian poet was describing his own metamorphosis into a poet-prophet.

A generation later, Victor Hugo penned his ode to the founder of Islam. Entitled 'The Ninth Year of the Hegira' (*L'an 9 de l'hégire*), it was published in

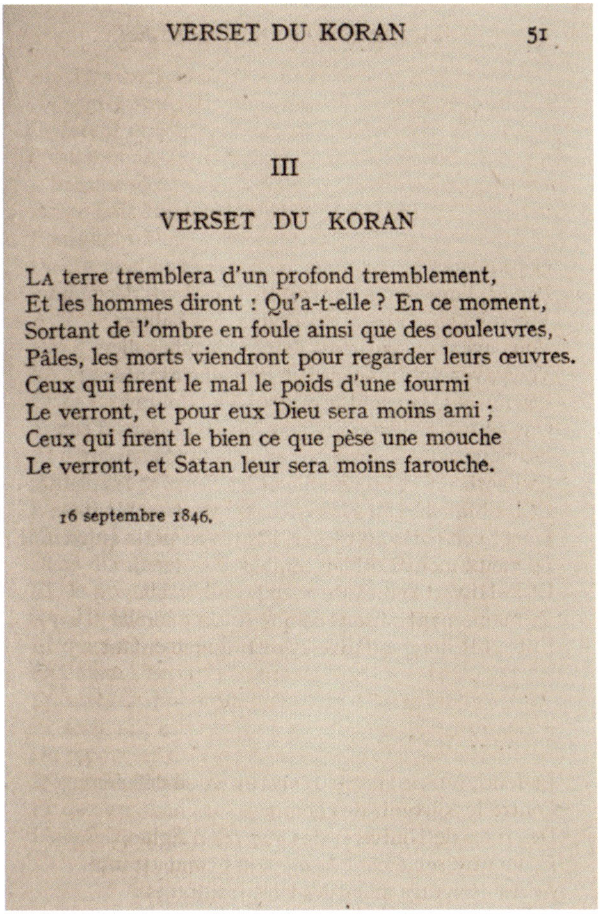

VERSET DU KORAN 51

III

VERSET DU KORAN

La terre tremblera d'un profond tremblement,
Et les hommes diront : Qu'a-t-elle ? En ce moment,
Sortant de l'ombre en foule ainsi que des couleuvres,
Pâles, les morts viendront pour regarder leurs œuvres.
Ceux qui firent le mal le poids d'une fourmi
Le verront, et pour eux Dieu sera moins ami ;
Ceux qui firent le bien ce que pèse une mouche
Le verront, et Satan leur sera moins farouche.

16 septembre 1846.

Fig. 5: Victor Hugo, *La Légende des Siècles*, vol. 2 (Paris, 1877), here in a later edition (Paris, 1912), 51

Hugo's first volume of his collection of epic poems, *La Légende des Siècles* (1858; **fig. 5**). The poem depicts Muhammad as a heroic leader, generous, wise, upright, welcoming death in modesty and contentment. Goethe's, Pushkin's, and Hugo's admiration for the Prophet reflects their own poetic-prophetic aspirations. Remarkably, each of them – arguably the greatest German, Russian, and French literary figures of their century – were moved to imitate Qurʾānic passages. Goethe, as already mentioned, discreetly included Qurʾānic verses in his *West-Eastern Divan*. Pushkin's engagement with the Qurʾān was sustained and explicit.

In 1826, he published a short collection of nine poems entitled 'Imitations of the Qurʾān' (*Podrazhaniia Koranu*). Hugo's lyrical rendition of Sura 99 entitled *Verset du Koran* appeared in the second volume of *La Légende des Siècles* (1877).

After the Romantics

The Qurʾān continued to offer a model for European mystical musings in the twentieth century. Rainer Maria Rilke (1875–1926) was driven to write his masterpiece *Duineser Elegien* ('The Duino Elegies', 1923), while studying the Muslim Scripture. In a letter from December 1912, he declares: 'I'm reading the Qurʾān, in place it takes on a voice for me, in which I'm immersed with all my strength, like the wind in the organ.' Referring to Goethe's *Mahomets Gesang*, he continues: 'like a river through an ancient mountain range, [Muhammad] breaks his way through to the one God.'[10] With the emergence of literary modernism, the aspect of the Muslim Scripture that had most baffled European readers – its non-linear, 'chaotic' structure – was reassessed and even celebrated. This fragmented nature of the Qurʾān enables a multiplicity of interpretations. It draws the reader into an enclosed textual universe with no beginning or end. James Joyce (1882–1941) aimed for a similar effect when writing his avant-garde novel *Finnegans Wake* (1939). A linguistic attempt to create a dream-like, non-linear narrative, Joyce's novel contains numerous explicit and implicit references to the Qurʾān. Among the former is a parody of the *basmala*, the ritual formula that opens the Qurʾānic suras. In place of 'In the name of Allah, the all-merciful, the most merciful,' Joyce writes, 'In the name of Annah the Allmaziful, the Everliving, the Bringer of Plurabilities!'

The great Argentinian writer, Jorge Luis Borges (1899–1986), a precursor of postmodernism, lingers on the Muslim Scripture in his playful exploration of the cult of books. Borges seems to have had the Qurʾān in mind when he conceived the short story *The Book of Sand*. The story focuses on the discovery of a magical scripture – 'the Book of Books' – with an infinite number of ever-changing elements, where 'no page is the first; none is the last.'

The Qurʾān was the object of sustained and productive attention by some of Europe's most important nineteenth and twentieth-century writers. The readings of Goethe, Pushkin, Hugo, Rilke, Joyce, and Borges of a scripture that had been, for centuries, feared, misunderstood, and vilified, were daring and pioneering. While the number of European writers who have productively engaged the Muslim Scripture is relatively modest, their stature is such that they irreversibly introduced the Qurʾān into European literary imagination.

1 Antoine Galland in his preface to Barthélemy d'Herbelot, *Bibliothèque Orientale*, 1776 [1697], viii.

2 The verses, known as the 'challenge' verses, are Q. 17:88; Q. 2:23; Q.10:38; Q. 11:13; Q. 28:49, and Q. 52:34.

3 The expression 'Alcoran chaos' was coined by the English scholar Samuel Purchas who authored a catalogue of religions of the world, entitled *Purchas, His Pilgrimage* (1613).

4 Voltaire in a letter ('There is a devil of an Englishman who made a very beautiful translation of the Alcoran.')

5 Goethe, *West-Eastern Divan: Complete, annotated new translation, including Goethe's "Notes and Essays" and the unpublished poems* (2019, London), 367–8. Translation by Eric Ormby, except for *erhaben*, which he translates as 'exalted'.

6 Letter from Boysen to Gleim (8 April 1745), *Briefe vom Herrn Boysen an Herrn Gleim* (Frankfurt and Leipzig, 1772), 38.

7 J.W. Goethe, *West-East Divan: The Poems, with 'Notes and Essays'*, translation by M. Bidney (Albany, 2010) 124.

8 Johann Gottfried Herder, 'Ueber die Wirkung der Dichtkunst auf die Sitten der Völker in alten und neuen Zeiten' ('On the Effect of Poetic Art on the Ethics of Peoples in Ancient and Modern Times', 1778), in *Sämtliche Werke*, (Karlsruhe, 1821), vol. 9, 368; translated by the author.

9 Alexander Pushkin, 'The Prophet' in *The Cambridge Companion to Pushkin*, (Cambridge, 2006) 30.

10 'Rilke's Duino Angels and the Angels of Islam', *Alif: Journal of Comparative Poetics*, 23 (2003), 191–211.

Colonialism and the Qurʾān

Omar Nasr, The London School of Economics and Political Science

Napoleon Bonaparte embarked on his expedition to Egypt in 1798. Equipped with Claude-Etienne Savary's latest French translation of the Qurʾān, he used the time aboard to familiarize himself with the religion of those he was about to conquer. Upon arriving in Egypt, he faced fierce resistance from the Egyptians, led by the scholars of al-Azhar University. In response, the French colonial authorities adopted a conciliatory strategy, heavily laced with Islamic rhetoric. French orientalists diligently read and interpreted the Qurʾān, moulding its messages to align with their colonial objectives. They also attempted to translate French proclamations into 'Qurʾānic Arabic to give religious legitimacy to the occupying regime.'[1] Even though the French noticed that Egyptian Muslims did not believe their claims of converting to Islam, memorising the Qurʾān, and planning to undergo circumcision, Bonaparte 'had an unappealing tendency to believe his own propaganda.'[2]

This article will show the multifaceted interconnections between colonialism and Europe's engagement with the Qurʾān. Challenging simplistic perceptions of how the Qurʾān and European colonial practices were (dis-)connected, I will provide a more nuanced understanding of the complex relationship between European colonialism and the use of the Qurʾān based on the case studies of British, French, Austro-Hungarian and German colonial traditions.[3]

The Qur᾿ān and the 'classical colonial powers': Britain and France[4]

Over the course of the nineteenth century, Europe's initial missionary and philological approaches to studying the Qur᾿ān were expanded by an 'axis joining scholarship and conquest'[5] amidst the rise of imperialism. The example of the Scottish orientalist and later principal of the University of Edinburgh, William Muir (d.1905), stands emblematic for this development. As lieutenant governor of the North-West Provinces of British India, Muir sparked public controversy when he declared that Muhammad was influenced by the Devil, coining the notion 'Satanic Verses' – around a century before Salman Rushdie – which even many British orientalists regarded as too radical.[6] For Muir, 'the sword of Mahomet, and the Coran are the most fatal enemies of Civilisation, Liberty and the Truth which the world has yet known.'[7] Representing a polemic and colonial school of orientalists who increasingly put their mostly theologically motivated scholarship in the service and justification of colonial administration, Muir serves as an epitome of Saidian critique of knowledge.[8]

Nevertheless, generalizing Muir's approach as applying to all European, or even all British orientalists would be an oversimplification. According to the British orientalist Humayun Ansari, writing about Islam and Muslims 'was never a unified and universally accepted project among British administrators and scholars'[9], emphasising internal debates and heterogenous positions regarding Islam. Still, we cannot deny that 'the dominant discourse dovetailed the colonialist experience'[10] in the late nineteenth and early twentieth British and French empires. As far as the British and French cases, in particular, are concerned, orientalists who hurried to defend their fields as 'pure scholarship' merely driven by 'Lust of Knowing', were not convincing.[11]

Edward Said's critique of – mainly British and French – orientalism became particularly influential as the sources from colonial archives were imbued with the unmistakable entanglement of knowledge production and colonial power structures. While there certainly was an exchange of orientalist knowledge between France and Britain, their practical applications of the Qur᾿ān differed with regard to colonial governance. British colonial rule is often seen as more liberal due to its practice of 'indirect rule', in contrast to France's 'mission civilisatrice'.[12] Examining their approaches to Islamic law and the Qur᾿ān reveals, however, that their distinction between direct and indirect rule was more nuanced, with the mode of ruling ultimately determined by the colonial powers' interests. The practical value Britain ascribed to the Qur᾿ān for colonial purposes becomes apparent in their *Anglo-Muhammedan Law*, 'a mixture of English and Islamic laws,

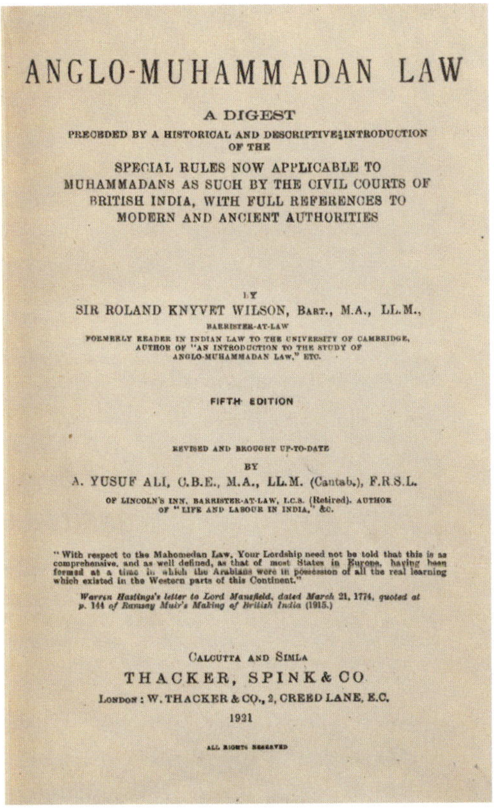

ANGLO-MUHAMMADAN LAW

A DIGEST

PRECEDED BY A HISTORICAL AND DESCRIPTIVE INTRODUCTION OF THE

SPECIAL RULES NOW APPLICABLE TO MUHAMMADANS AS SUCH BY THE CIVIL COURTS OF BRITISH INDIA, WITH FULL REFERENCES TO MODERN AND ANCIENT AUTHORITIES

BY

SIR ROLAND KNYVET WILSON, BART., M.A., LL.M.,

BARRISTER-AT-LAW

FORMERLY READER IN INDIAN LAW TO THE UNIVERSITY OF CAMBRIDGE, AUTHOR OF "AN INTRODUCTION TO THE STUDY OF ANGLO-MUHAMMADAN LAW," ETC.

FIFTH EDITION

REVISED AND BROUGHT UP-TO-DATE

BY

A. YUSUF ALI, C.B.E., M.A., LL.M. (Cantab.), F.R.S.L.

OF LINCOLN'S INN, BARRISTER-AT-LAW, I.C.S. (Retired), AUTHOR OF "LIFE AND LABOUR IN INDIA," &c.

"With respect to the Mahomedan Law, Your Lordship need not be told that this is as comprehensive, and as well defined, as that of most States in Europe, having been formed at a time in which the Arabians were in possession of all the real learning which existed in the Western parts of this Continent."

Warren Hastings's letter to Lord Mansfield, dated March 21, 1774, quoted at p. 144 of Ramsay Muir's Making of British India (1915.)

CALCUTTA AND SIMLA

THACKER, SPINK & CO

LONDON: W. THACKER & CO., 2, CREED LANE, E.C.

1921

ALL RIGHTS RESERVED

Fig. 1: First Page of the influential *Anglo-Muhammadan Law* by Roland Knyvet Wilson (London, 1895)

concepts, institutions, and jurisprudence,'[13] as the basis of state-Muslim relations in large swathes of the British Empire. A *Franco-Muhammadan Law* in line with the British version was only briefly attempted in French Marocco in the twentieth-century interwar period.[14]

In British colonial history, efforts in this direction began with the British East India Company (EIC), which from 1726 began legally intervening in local affairs. This initially entailed applying English law to both English people and natives until they declared that natives were no longer subject to English law in 1753. In 1772, the EIC introduced separate laws for Hindus and Muslims, which extended beyond trade and revenue: 'in all suits regarding inheritance, succession, marriage, and caste, and other religious usages or institutions, the laws of the

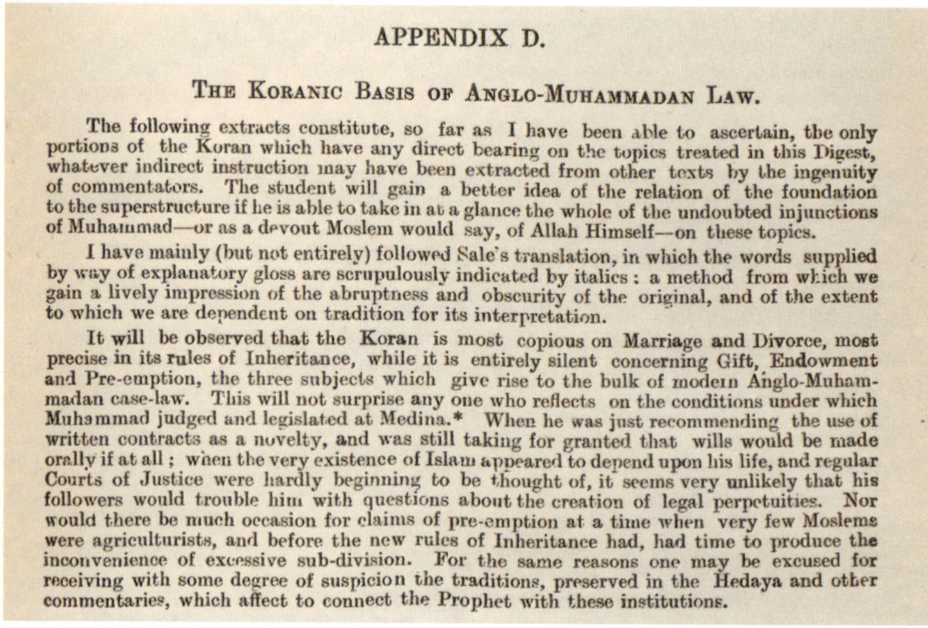

APPENDIX D.

THE KORANIC BASIS OF ANGLO-MUHAMMADAN LAW.

The following extracts constitute, so far as I have been able to ascertain, the only portions of the Koran which have any direct bearing on the topics treated in this Digest, whatever indirect instruction may have been extracted from other texts by the ingenuity of commentators. The student will gain a better idea of the relation of the foundation to the superstructure if he is able to take in at a glance the whole of the undoubted injunctions of Muhammad—or as a devout Moslem would say, of Allah Himself—on these topics.

I have mainly (but not entirely) followed Sale's translation, in which the words supplied by way of explanatory gloss are scrupulously indicated by italics: a method from which we gain a lively impression of the abruptness and obscurity of the original, and of the extent to which we are dependent on tradition for its interpretation.

It will be observed that the Koran is most copious on Marriage and Divorce, most precise in its rules of Inheritance, while it is entirely silent concerning Gift, Endowment and Pre-emption, the three subjects which give rise to the bulk of modern Anglo-Muhammadan case-law. This will not surprise any one who reflects on the conditions under which Muhammad judged and legislated at Medina.* When he was just recommending the use of written contracts as a novelty, and was still taking for granted that wills would be made orally if at all; when the very existence of Islam appeared to depend upon his life, and regular Courts of Justice were hardly beginning to be thought of, it seems very unlikely that his followers would trouble him with questions about the creation of legal perpetuities. Nor would there be much occasion for claims of pre-emption at a time when very few Moslems were agriculturists, and before the new rules of Inheritance had, had time to produce the inconvenience of excessive sub-division. For the same reasons one may be excused for receiving with some degree of suspicion the traditions, preserved in the Hedaya and other commentaries, which affect to connect the Prophet with these institutions.

Fig. 2: Appendix D in Wilson's book in which he lists and comments on the verses of the Qurʾān that form 'The Koranic Basis of Anglo-Muhammadan Law'. From Roland Knyvet Wilson, *A Digest of Anglo-Muhammadan Law* (London, 1895), 489

Koran with respect to Mohammedans … shall be invariably adhered to.'[15] This development continued well into the eighteenth and nineteenth centuries. In the early second millennium, a substantial colonial library of translations, codifications, and precedence cases had been established, forming the foundation of Anglo-Muhammadan law (**figs. 1, 2**). This law model was adopted in British West and East Africa, and in Palestine[16], with consideration given to variations in the dominant jurisprudential school encountered.[17] It should be noted, however, that Britain's colonial rule with shariʿa was not actually based on the text of the Qurʾān itself. As colonial authorities and orientalists arrived in the colonies, they found a disparity between the Qurʾānic text they had meticulously studied and de facto-practised law in the respective colony.

The question of whether the British should formulate an Anglo-Muhammedan law based on the Qurʾānic text or not became a matter of debate in the British colonial administration. The judgment of Sir Erskine Perry, a British judge in

Colonial India, gives insight into the position Britain eventually took towards this matter:

> If the meaning of this clause is that it is an absolute enactment or adoption of the Koran as of a positive unchangeable law, without regard to what the usages of India, whether Shia, Sunni, or sectarian, might have been undoubtedly the customs set up in conflict with the text of the Koran cannot be sustained. But I think it is quite clear that the clause in question was framed solely on political views, and without any reference to orthodoxy or the purity of any particular religious belief. ... But the policy which led to this clause proceeded upon the broad, easily recognisable basis of allowing the newly conquered people to retain their domestic usages. ... I am, therefore, clearly of opinion that the effect of the clause in the Charter is not to adopt the text of the Koran as law, any further than it has been adopted in the laws and usages of the Muhammadans who came under our sway; and if any class of Muhammadans, Muhammadan dissenters as they may be called, are found to be in possession of any usage which is otherwise valid as a legal custom, and which does not conflict with any express law of the English Government, they are just as much entitled to the protection of this clause as the most orthodox society which can come before the Court.[18]

This does not mean, however, that the British did not engage with the Qurʾānic text at all. In an effort to codify Islamic Law within the framework of the English legal tradition, Sir Roland Knyvet Wilson's influential 1895 treatise included an appendix entitled 'The Koranic Basis of Anglo-Muhammadan Law'. In this section, Wilson – an orientalist and professor of Indian Law at Cambridge University – lists the verses of the Qurʾān that he found relevant to this law. For this purpose, he relied mainly but not exclusively on the 1734 English translation of the Qurʾān by George Sale.[19]

In general, preference was given to translating widely-used fiqh (Islamic jurisprudence) manuals, such as *al-Hidaya* – a primary manual in Hanafi jurisprudence translated into English by Charles Hamilton in 1790 and mainly used for Britain's colonial rule in India. Another text predominantly used for colonial rule in West Africa was the *Mukhtasar* by Sidi Khalil, one of the most authoritative legal manuals in Maliki jurisprudence, widely applied in Northern Nigeria. In the preface to the 1916 English translation by the British orientalist

F.H. Ruxton, which he translated from a French version by French orientalist Perron soon after France took Algiers in 1830, Ruxton writes:

> The advantage to be gained to know something of the law of the people we govern is self-evident, especially when, as in the case of Muhammadan countries, it is the Law that has moulded the people, and not the people the Law ... The more we can grasp the inward significance of motives and acts, the more sympathetically, and therefore the more efficiently we shall be enabled to administer Muhammadan peoples.[20]

While Ruxton's translation primarily aimed at enabling colonial administrators to better understand, and thus indirectly rule, Muslims in northern Nigeria, Perron's original French translation of the *Mukhtasar* had a different purpose in Algeria. Perron's translation sought to identify which parts of Islamic law required 'replacement or modification to conform with French law,'[21] 'both for the good of the Colony and to foster the genesis and development among the Arabs of ideas more in harmony with those of the civilised world.'[22]

The case of France's colonial rule over Algeria illustrates a different approach to incorporating the Qurʾān into colonial law. French colonial authorities did not tolerate an independent Muslim judicial system; rather, they sought to subordinate it to the French courts. The office of the *qadi* – a state-appointed religious leader responsible for implementing Qurʾānic principles, which was the backbone of the Muslim judicial system – was 'decidedly altered.'[23] Furthermore, Islamic scholars, 'were deprived of the mainstay of their autonomy, the religious endowments ...'[24] This attitude towards religious affairs sparked early rejection and revolts against the colonial state. The office of the qadi, once regarded as the carrier and preserver of Qurʾānic rulings, became a mockery. As a group of Algerian Muslims jested, 'The qadis which the infidel will choose for us will sell justice for hard cash. What will become of the good Muhammadan law? The qadi will arrive drunk for the session.'[25]

The French, however, adapted their approach to the Qurʾān and Islamic law as needed. When France intensified its efforts to dominate Mauritania in the first decade of the twentieth century, Xavier Coppolani, the 'architect of Mauritania's colonization',[26] developed a plan of pacification outlined in his *politique des tribus*.[27] Unlike the secularisation approach found in other French colonies, France enforced and de-privatised Islamic Law in Mauretania, making it the colony's de facto law and regulating even the social lives of non-Muslims. The aim was to empower the religious Zawi qadis over the Hassan warriors, who were resisting the French, thereby securing the support of the Muslim elite, dividing and pacifying the Mauritanians, and establishing colonial power. Coppolani was seen as 'a friend of Muslims' (*il fut l'ami des musulmans*), as he had restored and spread the long-weakened Islamic legal system.[28]

A particularly cynical aspect of this policy was the imposition of *zakat* and *ushur* taxes, categorized as 'Qurʾānic taxes' (*impôts coraniques*) on Mauritanians. By 1905, these taxes comprised almost three quarters of the colonial budget in Mauritania and were considered 'the principal base of our fiscal regime in Mauritania'[29] by the French colonial administration. Unlike in Algeria, the Qurʾān and Islamic reasoning were not sidelined or secularised but appropriated by and for the colonial regime.

The Qurʾān in Austro-Hungarian and German colonialism

The Habsburg and German orientalist schools pursed a somewhat different approach to the Qurʾān and its practical use for colonial purposes.[30] In contrast to British and French colonial traditions, both Austro-Hungarian and German orientalism did not directly engage with the Qurʾānic text for colonial purposes. With the Habsburg occupation of Bosnia and Herzegovina in 1878, a large number of Austrian and Hungarian orientalists – such as Amand von Schweiger-Lerchenfeld (d.1910) and Adolf Strauss (d.1944) – published books on the land and people of Bosnia, including detailed studies on the role of the Qurʾān in the life of Bosnian Muslims.[31]

In Strausz's 1882 Bosnien, *Land und Leute* ('Bosnia: Land and People'), the chapter *Der Bosniake mohamedanischer Religion* ('The Bosniak of the Mohammedan Religion') portrayed the Qurʾān as governing all aspects of Bosnian Muslim life. According to Strauss, only 'what the Qurʾān prescribes is sacred to them; everything else is condemned and despised.' The Qurʾān was also seen as dangerous, as it incited 'the hatred the Qurʾān prescribes against non-believers' and was the main hindrance to any judicial progress, being the static source of law. Were it not for the Qurʾān, as Strauss concluded, the Bosnian Muslims would have had great potential, as they originally belonged to a 'noble class.'[32] In sum, Strauss argued that the Qurʾān corrupted Muslims and was the reason for the division between Muslims and other denominations. Due to the dark conditions brought about by the Ottomans and Islam, he noted, 'everyone was convinced that the time had come for a foreign power to intervene and, in whatever manner, bring peace and tranquillity to these unfortunate lands.'[33]

In his work Bosnien: *Das Land und seine Bewohner* ('Bosnia: The Land and its Inhabitants'), Amand von Schweiger-Lerchenfeld highlighted what he saw as the difference between the Austrian colonial government and other European governments. While other 'Christian empires of the Occident, like Russia, England, and France' ruled over Muslims, he argued that 'it is fundamentally different whether such peoples are merely externally connected to the central authority or fall within its immediate sphere of power and influence, as is specifically the case with the Bosnians under the Austro-Hungarian monarchy.' He asserted that the monarchy's goal should be to make 'all conditions and institutions' that are not Christian 'disappear', not by force but by *civilisatorische Bestrebungen* ('civilizational efforts'). For Islam, he saw only two options: 'either Islam allows itself to be modified in the spirit of *abendländische Culturarbeit* [Western cultural work], or it must cease to exist as a state factor with all its dogmatic prepotency.'[34]

Schweiger-Lerchenfeld, however, favoured the approach of modernisation, emphasising that despite the Qurʾān's suppression of the *Islamitin* ('the Muslim woman'), Bosnian Muslim men typically do not marry more than one woman. This practice, he argued, renders 'the whole harem-economy less dangerous' and elevates 'the Bosnian Muslim a level above his co-religionists in the Orient.' He further suggested that this would make the 'reform of Islam in Bosnia' easier for the state, a reform deemed 'necessary for the general state order,' even if it required years and had to be implemented 'gradually'.[35]

In other words, Austro-Hungarian orientalists viewed the Qurʾān as a constant looming threat that was responsible for the backwardness, stagnation, and division of Bosnia and Herzegovina. Andre Gingrich's concept of 'frontier orientalism', mainly focusing on Austrian orientalism, offers an explanation for this approach, demonstrating that 'the Oriental' was historically received as the 'Bad Muslim Oriental' due to the protracted conflicts with the Ottoman Empire and the entrenched image of 'the Turk'. The creation of a 'Good Muslim Oriental' was believed to be achievable only through rigid control, modification of his religion, and the consequent pacification and domestication. Despite these efforts, the Muslim was always seen as inherently possessing the potential to be dangerous, a trait perceived as intrinsic to the Qurʾān. Consequently, Muslims had to remain under constant surveillance and be treated with persistent suspicion.[36]

The Austrian policy to Islam aimed at distancing Bosnian Muslims from Ottoman cultural and religious traditions and institutions. Therefore, Austria unofficially encouraged Bosnian Muslims 'to propose their own religious leadership, separate from the Ottoman authorities.' This led to the establishment of

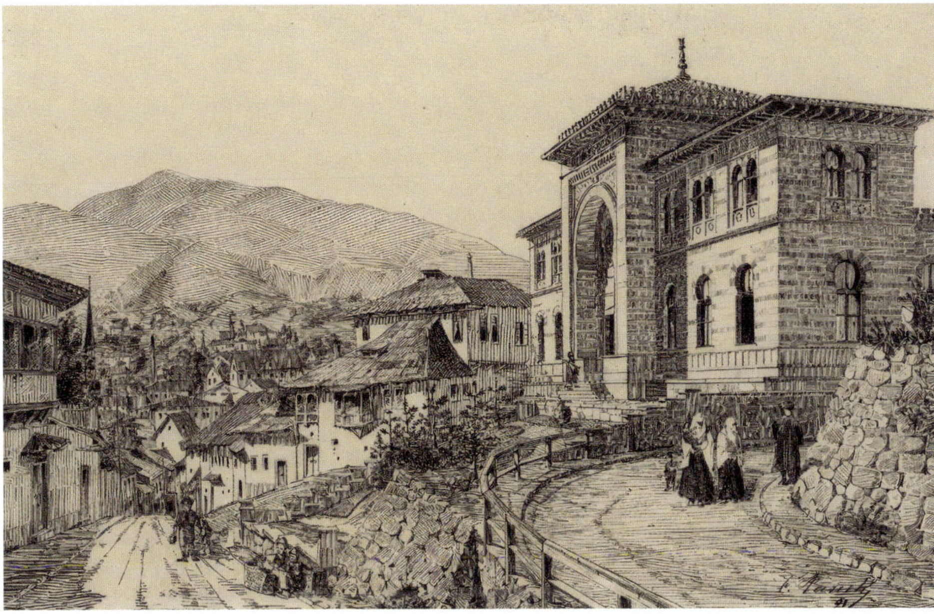

Fig. 3: The *Scheriatrichterschule* (Islamic Law School) in Sarajevo was opened in 1889 and played a crucial role in the Austro-Hungarian policy towards Bosnian Muslims. The school was built in a distinguished Moorish architectural design by the prominent Czech architect Karel Pařík. Vienna, Austrian National Library, PK 1131, 1564

the '*reis ul-ulema* at its helm' and 'an advisory council, *medžlis-i ulema*' ('council of scholars'), and the installation of a grand mufti in 1887.[37] Additionally, an Islamic Law School (*Scheriatrichterschule*), built in Andalusian architectural design to forge a distinct Islamic cultural tradition for Bosnian Muslims, was opened in 1889.[38] Rather than studying Islam in Istanbul, Bosnian Muslims were now encouraged to study at the *Scheriatrichterschule*, allowing them to learn their religion 'in their own language' while also acquiring proficiency in German.[39] Graduates were appointed as *qadis*, operating under the office of the *reis ul-ulema*, established by the monarchy. Consequently, Islamic Law was not sidelined but rather transformed, 'resulting in a unique blend of Ottoman Islamic legal practices and Habsburg legal structures and values' (see **fig. 3**).[40]

In 1912, Austria issued an Islam Act concerning 'the recognition of followers of Islam according to the Hanafi rite as a religious community'.[41] This law elevated Islam to the status of a recognised religious community (*Religionsgesellschaft*), but it specifically acknowledged only the Hanafi jurisprudential tradition, which was perceived to be more compatible with European values, particularly regarding polygamy. The law was part 'of long-standing efforts to domesticate Muslims by cutting them off from their transnational ties to the Ottoman Caliphate at the time and making them loyal to the Austro-Hungarian Empire.'[42] The 1912 Islam Act remained in effect even after the collapse of the Habsburg Empire and was only thoroughly revised by the Austrian government in 2014 under protest by Austrian Muslims.[43]

A striking continuity of this policy and its underlying frontier orientalist suspicion towards Islam is evident in one of the proposed features for the revised 2014 Islam Act. This unprecedented proposal, not only within the Austrian context but also across all European colonial traditions, called for an *Einheitsübersetzung* of the Qur'ān – a uniform translation intended to serve as the foundation for state-Muslim relations. In an interview, then-chancellor Sebastian Kurz elucidated his rationale, stating, 'There are countless translations, countless interpretations of the Qur'ān', and emphasising that 'the majority population deserves to know what the content of the faith is.'[44] Although this proposal was ultimately not incorporated into the new law, the revised legislation did lead to the establishment of an Islamic theological institute at the University of Vienna, encouraging future Imams to pursue their studies and training in Austria rather than abroad, thereby continuing the historical policy of domesticating Muslims.[45]

Utilising knowledge of Islam and the Qur'ān for colonial purposes departed clearly from a long-standing philological tradition epitomised by scholars like Ignaz Goldziher (d.1921) and Theodor Nöldeke (d.1930).[46] Nonetheless, these orientalists are still sometimes charged with 'epistemic colonialism' and 'Eurocentric intellectual totalitarianism', such as in the recent article on *Decolonizing Qur'ānic Studies* by Joseph Lumbard, due to their belief that Muslim 'methodologies are epistemically inferior to the methodologies of the modern Euro-American scholar', leading to a dismissal of the traditional Muslim disciplines of *tafsir* studies and *ulum al-qur'an*.[47]

In clear contrast to the philological orientalist tradition, such orientalists as Schweiger-Lerchenfeld and Strauss, as well as the German orientalists Carl Heinrich Becker (d.1933), Martin Hartmann (d.1918) and Georg Kampffmeyer (d.1936) directly engaged in colonial practice and produced knowledge specifically catered for colonial purposes. This shift is captured in Kampffmeyer's 1913 article in the journal *Die Welt des Islam*, where he discusses the 'partial transformation of our oriental scholarship' towards the 'doing of useful things', questioning, 'Who should study the conditions in our colonies if not us?'[48] This approach marks the departure from a Humboldtian concept of *Wissenschaft* to the pragmatic approach of *Nutzbarkeit* during the era of Wilhelmine *Weltpolitik*.[49]

Unlike the Austrians, however, German orientalists engaged more extensively with Islamic jurisprudential literature in German East Africa. This is evident in the numerous writings of C.H. Becker, who devoted much of his scholarship to the study of Islam in German East Africa.[50] He cynically criticised orientalists who were surprised that 'an Islam, as one might construct based on the Qurʾān, is entirely unknown throughout the country', adding that this is not only the case in German East Africa, but 'one would search in vain for such an Islam anywhere in the world.'[51] Instead, he preferred a more anthropological approach, observing the behaviour of Muslims and analysing incident reports. Regarding literary materials, Becker suggested inquiring: 'Which books find their way into the hands of the local Mwalimus [religious preachers/teachers] and directly influence the intellectual life of our colony?'[52] To explore this question, he meticulously analysed six complete personal libraries of local religious leaders that had been confiscated by the German colonial administration, who subsequently granted him access.[53]

This crucial difference is also reflected in their distinct governing practices. While the Habsburg monarchy aimed at producing a version of Islam that suited their needs and loyal Muslim subjects, the Germans focused on understanding the religious texts to govern Islam, employing both 'positive measures' and 'tolerant non-interference'.[54] In contrast, the two options Austro-Hungarian orientalists suggested were that Islam should either 'be modified' or 'cease to exist as a state factor.'[55]

While both Austro-Hungarian and German colonial policies towards Islam differ to some extent from Britain and France, a learning process from them cannot be overlooked. Perhaps not to the extent that Edward Said suggested when he asserted that 'the major steps in oriental scholarship were first taken in either Britain and France, then elaborated upon by Germans.'[56] As Britain and France had a longer colonial tradition, Austrian and German scholars and orientalists used their experience for academic explorations and contributed to the respective colonial projects of mainly Britain and France. More importantly, however, German and Austrian colonial officials and their orientalists studied these French and British models.[57] More directly, Habsburg officials held meetings with British colonial officers, seeking to learn from their colonial experiences due to the 'similarity of governmental tasks'.[58]

The Qur'ān in colonial war propaganda

In World War I, German orientalists led by Max von Oppenheim advised Kaiser Wilhelm II that Islam could be instrumentalised to destabilise France and Britain. They convinced him that the Ottoman sultan could rally Muslims against the Entente powers by issuing a call to jihad. Sultan Mehmed V issued such a decree in November 1914, followed by the Bosnian *reis-ul-ulema* Džemaludin Čaušević, and targeting mainly Russia, England, and France. After all, the jihad-propaganda of World War I had a larger impact on the Triple Entente than on Muslims themselves. As Eugene Rogan notes, the threat of jihad was the main reason for Britain to deepen its engagement in the Middle Eastern theatre. 'Ironically', he emphasises, 'the British proved more responsive to the Ottoman call to jihad than the global Muslim community.'[59]

After Germany's defeat in World War I, the interwar years were marked by Germany's longing for the return of the glorious years of the Wilhelminian Empire.[60] These nostalgic sentiments were embraced by Hitler in his grandiose dreams of Nazi expansion. In the course of World War II, the Third Reich dominated a considerable number of Muslims in the Balkans, the Caucasus, and briefly in North Africa. In the wake of total mobilisation and with the advice of German orientalists – some of whom had already served in World War I, such as Max von Oppenheim – the Nazis utilised the Qur'ān in their propaganda efforts to court and win over Muslims and destabilise the Allied colonial powers.[61]

The British Empire, in response, decided on a large-scale propaganda strategy with one strand concerned with 'selling democracy' to Muslims throughout the Arab world.[62] This publicity campaign aimed to stress the similarities between the Allied commitment to democracy and the Islamic worldview, particularly the Qur'ānic principle of *shura* ('consultation'). A British propaganda poster read: 'The religion of Islam is the spirit of democracy' and 'Democracy is the essence of the Qur'ān and Islamic teaching; its triumph would be the final triumph of the principles of Islam.'[63]

As a particular feature, both Axis and Allied powers competed to reach Muslims through broadcasting the Qur'ān. When the British noticed the bad quality of German Qur'ān broadcastings, they decided for a strategy that aimed to not 'use Koran as a bait, but to give it in a dignified context as a principle item in our programmes.'[64] Their strategy focused on providing high-quality content by recruiting 'the finest readers in the Moslem world' and forming 'the nucleus of a library, which will enable us ... to give regular recitals of the Koran ... '[65]

Eventually, as the British themselves noted regarding their Qur'ān recitation

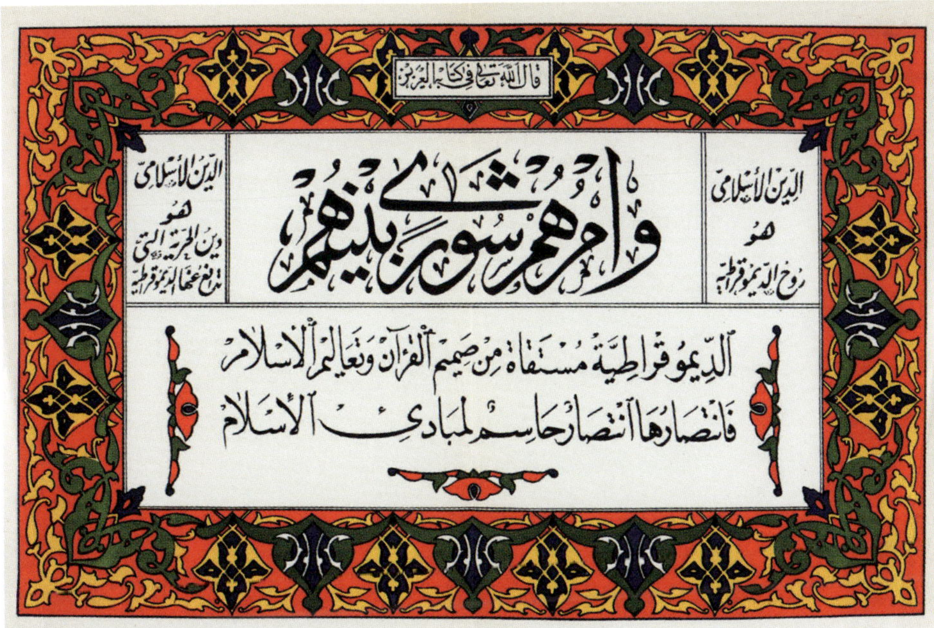

Fig. 4: A British propaganda poster displaying a verse from the Qurʾān (48:27) and Arabic slogans promoting the compatibility between Islam and democracy to counter Fascist propaganda during World War II. London, The National Archives, sig. INF 2/36

programme: 'this device of using the Koran … does not deceive the majority of our listeners, who regard it as a rather base use of Holy Writ – the Devil quoting Scripture for his purposes.'[66] The vast majority of Muslims around the world did not regard the colonial powers' sudden awakening to Islam as sincere and continued to build allegiances with any power involved in the two war wars based on their own political and strategic interests, rather than on easily discernible propaganda (see **fig. 4**).[67]

Conclusion

Through the lens of the Qurʾān, this article set out to reveal some of the many sometimes divergent, sometimes convergent connections between different colonial projects and the Qurʾān in the imperial age. The relationship between orientalism, the Qurʾān, and colonialism is complex and multifaceted. Certainly, it is essential to study the numerous instances where orientalism and colonialism were intertwined as well as the lasting impact this had. Even in these many cases, however, generalisations would distort the varied orientalisms and their evolving relationships with the various forms of European colonialisms at play.

A glimpse at the proceedings of the International Congress of Orientalists reveals that while many participants were from colonial powers, many of them did not put their scholarship in the service of colonialism; and other orientalists came from European countries which did not have any colonies. Shortly after the inauguration of the congress in 1873, delegations of Muslim scholars and intellectuals from Muslim countries participated, transforming the congress into a 'space for the circulation of knowledge'.[68] As one participant of the congress expressed: 'We of the twentieth century come together ... not so much that we may read and listen to learned papers, as that we may see each other face to face and recognise that we are fellow-workers at the noble task of helping the East and the West to understand each other and so to respect each other, and so to live in peace and goodwill together.'[69]

1 David Motadel (ed.), *Islam and the European Empires* (Oxford, 2014), 5.

2 Juan Ricardo Cole, *Napoleon's Egypt: Invading the Middle East* (Basingstoke, 2008), 128.

3 For a trans-imperial study of Islam in European colonialism, see Motadel 2014 (see note 1) or Jane Burbank and Frederick Cooper, *Empires in World History: Power and the Politics of Difference* (Princeton, 2010).

4 The categorisation of Britain, France, and also the Netherlands as 'classical colonial powers' can be found in: Andre Gingrich, 'Frontier Myths of Orientalism: The Muslim World in Public and Popular Cultures of Central Europe', in *Mediterranean Ethnological Summer School*, 1998, 100.

5 Ziad Elmarsafy, 'Translations of the Qurʾān into Western Languages', *Religion Compass* 3 (May 2009), 434.

6 Avril A. Powell, *Scottish Orientalists and India: the Muir Brothers, Religion, Education and Empire* (Boydell & Brewer, 2010), 168; Clinton Bennett, Victorian Images of Islam (Piscataway, NJ, 1992), 103–27.

7 See William Muir, *The Life of Mahomet* (London, 1861), iv, 322.

8 Edward Said discussed Muir briefly in *Orientalism*; see Edward W. Said, Orientalism (New York, 1978), 151.

9 Humayun K. Ansari, 'The Muslim World in British Historical Imaginations: "Re-thinking Orientalism"?' *British Journal of Middle Eastern Studies* 38 (2011), 1, 93.

10 Ibid.

11 Bernard Lewis, 'The Question of Orientalism', *The New York Review of Books*, 29/11 (24 June 1982), 49–56; see Said's response and discussion: Edward W. Said and Oleg Grabar, 'Orientalism: An Exchange', *The New York Review of Books*, 29/13 (29 August 1982), https://www.nybooks.com/articles/1982/08/12/orientalism-an-exchange/ (accessed 25 July 2024).

12 See for a discussion: Frederick Cooper, *Colonialism in Question. Theory, Knowledge, History* (Berkeley, 2005).

13 Muhammad Khalid Masud, "Anglo-Muhammadan Law", in Kate Fleet et al. (eds.), *Encyclopaedia of Islam* 3 (2009), https://doi.org/10.1163/1573-3912_ei3_COM_22716 (accessed 25 July 2024).

14 Ari David Schriber, "The End of Sharīʿa? Adjudicating the Moroccan-Mālikī Legal Tradition in Colonial-Era Morocco (1921–56)", Ph.D. diss., Harvard University Graduate School of Arts and Sciences, 2021, 284. Some argue that Austria's 1912 Islam Act was perhaps inspired by Great Britain, see: Suzanne L. Marchand, *German Orientalism in the Age of Empire: Religion, Race, and Scholarship* (Washington, D.C., Cambridge, and New York, 2009), 334.

15 Masud 2009 (see note 13).

16 Ibid.; See also: Nhat-Dang Do and Michael Provence, "The Legitimacy of Repression: The History of Martial Law in British Controlled Palestine", *Equilibrium* 2, no. 1 (2016), 17–29.

17 In British Malaya, however, British policy towards Muslims was more complex. For an overview, see the chapter on "Islam and Colonisation" in: Syed Muhd Khairudin Aljunied, *Islam in Malaysia: An Entwined History, Religion and Global Politics* (New York, 2019), 107–29.

18 Roland Knyvet Wilson, *A Digest of Anglo–Muhammadan Law* (London, 1895), 334–5.

19 Ibid., 489.

20 Fitz Herbert Ruxton, *Maliki Law: Being a Summary from French Translations of the Mukhtasar of Sidi Khalil* (London, 1916), v.

21 Ibid., 4.

22 Ibid., 5.

23 Allan Christelow, *Muslim Law Courts and the French Colonial State in Algeria* (Princeton, 1985), 262.

24 Ibid.

25 Ibid., 265.

26 Abbas Braham, *Colonizing Shari'a: Islamic and Customary Law, the French Secular, and the Zwaya Ascendency in Mauritania, c.1900–40* (Tucson, AZ, 2020), 137.

27 See: Xavier Coppolani, *Mauritanie Saharienne: novembre 1903 à mai 1904* (Paris, 1999).

28 Cécile Frébourg, 'Coppolani revisité', *Revue Française de l'Histoire d'Outre-Mer*, 80 (1993), 615–26.

29 See: Braham 2020 (see note 26), 154.

30 Academics used various terms to describe the Habsburg's rule over Bosnia and

Herzegovina, such as 'semi-' and 'quasi-colony', or 'proximate colony'. This essay will use the shorthand designation of 'colony' for better readability. See for a discussion: Cooper 2005 (see note 12).

31 See a list of works published around 1878: ANNO (ÖNB),'Literatur-Bericht. Publicationen über Bosnien und die Hercegowina', in: *Österreichische Monatsschrift für den Orient*, 1 (15 January 1876), 128.

32 Adolf Strausz, *Bosnien, Land und Leute. Historisch-Ethnographisch-Geographische Schilderung* (Vienna, 1882), 175–206.

33 Ibid., 175–206, iv.

34 Amand von Schweiger-Lerchenfeld, *Bosnien, Das Land und seine Bewohner. Geschichtlich, geographisch, ethnographisch und social-politisch* (Vienna, 1878), 145.

35 Ibid., 131.

36 See: Andre Gingrich, 'Frontier Myths of Orientalism: The Muslim World in Public and Popular Cultures of Central Europe', *Mediterranean Ethnological Summer School*, 1998, 101, 119.

37 Leyla Amzi-Erdoğdular, *Afterlife of Empire: Muslim-Ottoman Relations in Habsburg Bosnia Herzegovina*, 1878–1914 (Stanford, 2024), 121.

38 See: Maximilian Hartmuth, 'Forging a Habsburg Muslim Elite: The Architecture of the Islamic Law School (Scheriatsrichterschule) in Sarajevo, 1887–1889', in Markus Ritter and Nourane Ben Azzouna (eds.), *Beiträge zur Islamischen Kunst und Archäologie*, vol. 8 (2022), 51–66.

39 Amzi-Erdoğdular 2024 (see note 37), 121.

40 See: Ninja Bumann, 'Forging a Habsburg Islamic Legal System: Legal Transformation and Local Agency in Habsburg Bosnia and Herzegovina (1878–1918)', *Journal of Islamic Law. Special Issue 'The Dynamics of Islamic Law with the Rise of Modernity'* 4/1 (2023), 51–92, here 51.

41 The 1912 Islam Act has been analysed thoroughly, also from a post-colonial perspective. See for example: Farid Hafez, 'Alte Neue Islampolitik in Österreich? Eine Postkoloniale Analyse der Österreichischen Islampolitik', *Zeitschrift Für Politik* 65/1 (2018), 22–44.

42 See: Farid Hafez, 'Criminalising Muslim Political Agency from Colonial Times to Today: The Case of Austria', in Naved Bakali and Farid Hafez (eds.), *The Rise of Global Islamophobia in the War on Terror* (Manchester, 2022), 97.

43 Farid Hafez, 'Austrian Muslims Protest Against Austria's Revised "Islam Act"', *Journal of Muslim Minority Affairs* 37/3 (3 July 2017), 267–83.

44 'Kurz für einheitliche Koran-Übersetzung', *Kurier*, 20 Sept. 2024, https://kurier.at/politik/inland/kurz-fuer-einheitliche-koran-uebersetzung/86.827.235 (accessed 15 July 2024).

45 See for an analysis: Rijad Dautović and Farid Hafez, 'Institutionalizing Islam in Contemporary Austria: A Comparative Analysis of the Austrian Islam Act of 2015 and Austrian Religion Laws with Special Emphasis on the Israelite Act of 2012', *Oxford Journal of Law and Religion* 8/1 (1 February 2019), 28–50.

46 See recently: Hans-Jürgen Becker et al. (eds.), 'Building Bridges: Ignaz Goldziher and His Correspondents, Islamic and Jewish Studies around the Turn of the Twentieth Century', *Islamic History and Civilization*, vol. 212 (Leiden and Boston, 2024). For a recent, more critical take, see: Katalin Franciska Rac, 'Arabic Literature for the Colonizer and the Colonized: Ignaz Goldziher and Hungary's Eastern Politics (1878–1918)', in Susannah Heschel and Umar Ryad (eds.), *The Muslim Reception of European Orientalism: Reversing the Gaze* (London, 2018).

47 Joseph Lumbard, 'Decolonizing Qurʾānic Studies', Religions 13/2 (17 Feb. 2022), 3–7.
48 Georg Kampffmeyer, 'Plane Perspicere', *Die Welt des Islams* 1/1 (1913), 1–6.
49 See: Suzanne L. Marchand, *German Orientalism in the Age of Empire* (Cambridge, 2009), 333–86, here 333.
50 See also a recent study focusing on C.H. Becker's contribution to the Austrian colonial experience in Bosnia and Herzegovina: Rifet Rustemović, 'Between the Sovereignty, State-Control and Non-Interference in Religion. The Islamic Community and the Muslims of Bosnia and Herzegovina in the Antithesis of the German Orientalist Carl Heinrich Becker (1876–1933)', *Prilozi Za Orijentalnu Filologiju* 72/72 (12 Nov. 2023), 261–300.
51 Carl Heinrich Becker, 'Materialien Zur Kenntnis des Islam in Deutsch-Ostafrika', *Der Islam; Zeitschrift für Geschichte und Kultur des Islamischen Orients* 2 (1911).
52 Ibid., 19.
53 Ibid., 18–41.
54 Carl Heinrich Becker , 'Islampolitik', *Die Welt des Islams* 3/2 (1915), 101.
55 Schweiger-Lerchenfeld 1878 (see note 34), 145.
56 Edward W. Said, *Orientalism* (New York, 1978), 17.
57 Ulrike Kirchberger, 'Between Transimperial Networking and National Antagonism: German Scientists in the British Empire during the Long Nineteenth Century', in Andrew Goss (eds.), *The Routledge Handbook of Science and Empire* (London, 2015), 144.
58 Amzi-Erdoğdular 2024 (see note 37), 118.
59 Eugene Rogan, 'Rival Jihads: Islam and the Great War in the Middle East, 1914–1918', *Journal of the British Academy* 4 (2016), 18.
60 See: Wolfe W. Schmokel: *Dream of Empire: German Colonialism 1919–1945.* (New Haven and London, 1964); Joachim Zeller, Ulrich van der Heyden: ... *Macht und Anteil an der Weltherrschaft. Berlin und der deutsche Kolonialismus.* (Münster, 2005).
61 See: David Motadel, *Islam and Nazi Germany's War* (Cambridge, MS, and London, 2014).
62 See Stefanie Wichhart, 'Selling Democracy During the Second British Occupation of Iraq, 1941–5', *Journal of Contemporary History* 48/3 (July 2013), 509–36. See also: Stefanie Wichhart, '"What Britain Has Done for Islam": British Propaganda to the Islamic World During World War II, 1939–1942', in Justin Quinn Olmstead (ed.), *Britain in the Islamic World* (Cham, 2019), 197–223.
63 *The National Archives of the United Kingdom*, INF 2/36. Also see Wichhart's article on this material (2013).
64 TNA, CO 323/1651/9, Broadcasting B.B.C Empire Broadcast Service: *Use of Foreign Languages*, 1939.
65 Ibid.
66 Ibid.
67 For a broader trans-imperial perspective on the instrumentalisation of Islam in both world wars, see: Xavier Bougarel, Raphaëlle Branche, and Cloé Drieu (eds.), *Combatants of Muslim Origin in European Armies in the Twentieth Century: Far from Jihad* (London, 2017).
68 Kapil Raj, 'Networks of Knowledge, or Spaces of Circulation? The Birth of British Cartography in Colonial South Asia in the Late Eighteenth Century', *Global Intellectual History* 2/1 (2 January 2017), 49–66.
69 Dandekar, R. N. 'The Twenty-First International Congress of Orientalists, Paris 23rd to 31st of July 1948.' *Annals of the Bhandarkar Oriental Research Institute* 29, no. 1/4 (1948), v.

This book is published on the occasion of the exhibition *The European Qurʾān*.

Weltmuseum Wien
www.weltmuseumwien.at
18 September 2024 to 24 August 2025

Director General
KHM-Museumsverband
Sabine Haag

Director Weltmuseum Wien
Jonathan Fine

Research for this volume was undertaken within the framework of the Synergy Grant Project 'The European Qurʾān. Islamic Scripture in European Culture and Religion 1150–1850 (EuQu)', which is funded by the European Research Council (ERC) in the framework of 'Horizon 2020: EU Programme for Research and Innovation' (grant agreement no. 810141).

Exhibition

Curators
Jan Loop
Naima Afif
Tobias Mörike

Curatorial Assistant
Kentaro Inagaki

Exhibition management
Elisabeth Kainberger

Exhibition design
Gerhard Veigel

Sponsors

welt museum wien friends

This publication was financially supported by Weltmuseum Wien Friends.

Publication

Edited by
Jan Loop
Naima Afif

Editorial coordination
Rafael Kopper

Copy editor
Daniel Stevens

Graphic design
Marianne Stålhös

Image rights and coordination
Ramona Heinlein

Image editing
Daniel Sostaric

ISBN 978-3-68924-182-7
e-ISBN (PDF) 978-3-68924-025-7

Library of Congress Control Number: 2024943791

Bibliographic information published by the Deutsche Nationalbibliothek
The Deutsche Nationalbibliothek lists this publication in the Deutsche Nationalbibliografie; detailed bibliographic data are available on the Internet at http://dnb.dnb.de.

Printed in the European Union.

Image credits

Cover: Marwan Shahin, *God is Perfect (Portrait of Johann Wolfgang von Goethe)*, 2024 © Marwan Shahin

Archivo Histórico Provincial de Málaga: 42
Bayerische Staatsbibliothek München: 16, 47, 62, 101
Biblioteca de Castilla-La Mancha: 43
Bibliothèque nationale de France: 13, 24, 27
Biblioteca Tomás Navarro Tomás. CSIC: 44
Fonds de dotation de l'Imprimerie Nationale: 84
KHM-Museumsverband: 57
Halle, Franckesche Stiftungen: 61
Leiden University Libraries: 86
Lithuania, Alytus, private collection: 50
Österreichische Nationalbibliothek Wien: 19, 59, 90, 91, 105, 119
Public Domain: 69, 70, 72, 74, 77, 79, 80, 107, 113, 114
Real Academia de la Historia. España: 41, 45
Rostock University Library: 14, 89
SLUB Dresden: 88
The National Archives (UK): 123
The Royal Danish Royal Library: 11
Universitätsbibliothek Leipzig: 96
Universitäts- und Landesbibliothek Sachsen-Anhalt: 20
Yakub Kolas Central Scientific Library of the National Academy of Sciences of Belarus: 48
Weimar, Goethe- und Schiller-Archiv, Foto: Klassik Stiftung Weimar: 102
Wien Museum: 56